ARTISTS
AND THEIR PETS

Library of Congress Cataloging-in-Publication Data available upon
request.
ISBN: 978-1-9460-6401-1

duopress books are available at special discounts when purchased in
bulk for sales promotions as well as for fund-raising or educational use.
Special editions can be created to specification. Contact us at
hello@duopressbooks.com for more information.

Manufactured in China
10 9 8 7 6 5 4 3 2

Duopress LLC
8 Market Place, Suite 300
Baltimore, MD 21202

Distributed by Workman Publishing Company, Inc.
Published simultaneously in Canada by Thomas Allen & Son Limited.

To order: hello@duopressbooks.com
www.duopressbooks.com
www.workman.com

ARTISTS

AND THEIR

PETS

by
SUSIE HODGE

art by
VIOLET LEMAY

dp
duopress

CONTENTS

iNTRODUCTiON

For centuries, artists all around the world have
enjoyed the company of pets, allowing animals'
calming influence and companionship to help them
concentrate on their work. You might be surprised
at how many artists do not always care for the
company of other humans, but many are real
animal lovers. Some, such as Pablo Picasso, Frida
Kahlo, Norman Rockwell, Andy Warhol,
and David Hockney, have used their artistic
talents to capture their pets' individual personalities
and characteristics. Others, such as Wassily
Kandinsky and René Magritte, painted many
unexpected things, but not their beloved pets.
Suzanne Valadon and Ai Weiwei simply

delighted when cats and other animals wandered into their homes. In all cases, these animals were treated with great respect.

Because so many artists have not led what most people consider to be "normal" lives, many have welcomed animals as their companions, as animals do not judge or criticize but offer unconditional, unquestioning love.

Here are just some examples of the great artists and their awesome pets you will find in this book: The Spanish artist Pablo Picasso was a great animal lover. Over his 91 years, he shared his home with umpteen different pets, including owls, dogs, a mouse, and a goat. The Mexican painter Frida Kahlo had a difficult time with her health and her husband, but her dogs, birds, monkeys, and fawn (called Granizo) loved her without judgment. Several other artists, such as Andy Warhol and Gustav Klimt, had a number of pets—usually independent cats—that wandered freely around their homes and studios, crumpling drawings and paintings to make themselves comfy beds. The American painter Jackson Pollock was often depressed, but as he made huge drip paintings, his dogs kept him company and made him feel happier.

Another American artist, Georgia O'Keeffe, liked peace and quiet as she worked, but she also liked the peace to be filled with the gentle purrs of her Siamese cats or the soft snores of her chow dogs. Romare Bearden, who was a social worker as well as an artist, was a great big man— with a great big heart, for people and his cats.

Yet while most of the artists in this book truly loved animals, Salvador Dalí preferred pets that drew attention to him. His animals became an extension of his extraordinary art. He was once photographed taking an anteater for a walk.

Dalí had two pet ocelots (or dwarf leopards) that he took with him to expensive hotels, art galleries, and restaurants. People worried about the ocelots because they could be dangerous, so he once told a woman in a restaurant that his ocelot was really a house cat that he had painted to look like an exotic jungle cat. As Dalí was so extravagant, the woman believed him.

Now read on to find out more about great artists and their awesome pets!

PABLO PICASSO

SPANISH MAESTRO

Probably the most influential
artist of the 20th century, the
Spanish artist Pablo Picasso had
a career that lasted for more than
75 years and enough pets to run
his own zoo!

One of the most prolific artists in the history of modern art, Pablo Picasso became a big name in art in the 20th century. He also had a big name: Pablo Diego José Francisco de Paula Juan Nepomuceno María de los Remedios Cipriano de la Santísima Trinidad Martyr Patricio Clito Ruíz y Picasso.

Picasso worked as a painter, sculptor, printmaker, ceramicist, and stage designer, and he produced thousands of works. Early in his career, however, he was so poor that he burned his drawings to keep warm.

Picasso was exceptionally skilled in art from a young age—which is known as being a child prodigy. His mother, Maria, said that his first word was "piz," short for *lápiz*, the Spanish word for pencil. Picasso's dad, José, bred pigeons and painted pictures of them, but he was unsuccessful as an artist, so he earned his living as an art teacher. He gave Pablo his first art lessons. Like his dad, Pablo also loved birds and often kept them later in life.

When he was 10, Pablo and his family moved from Malaga, where he was born, to La Coruña in northwest Spain. There he had his first pet dog, Clipper. Three years later, he painted Clipper's portrait.

Clipper

At 13, Pablo took a test to enter an art school in Barcelona. He completed (and passed) the test, which usually took older students a week, in an afternoon. At 16, he went to Spain's top art school in Madrid, but he spent most of his time in the Prado museum studying famous Spanish paintings.

In 1900, Picasso went to Paris with his dog Gat (Catalan for "cat"), which had been given to him by his friend Miguel Utrillo. Four years later, he moved into a building known as Bateau-Lavoir (Laundry-Boat) in Montmartre in Paris. There, as well as Gat, he had a cat, Mimiche, a tame white mouse, and two more dogs, Feo and Fricka, and he fed stray cats nearby. His pets kept him company, and he became friends with the city's most well-known artists, poets, and art dealers. In 1905, the American collectors Gertrude and Leo Stein began buying his work.

After his friend died in 1901, Picasso painted sad-looking pictures in shades of blue. From 1905 to 1906, he painted slightly happier pinkish pictures of circus characters. These became known as his Blue and Rose Periods respectively.

In 1907, Picasso saw African masks in a Paris museum and an exhibition of paintings by Paul Cézanne, who had died the year before. He used ideas from these experiences to create a large painting, unlike anything that had been seen before. *Les Demoiselles d'Avignon* shocked many, but it became one of the most important paintings of the 20th century.

With his friend Georges Braque, Picasso began experimenting with a new style of painting. He painted people, musical instruments, and other objects, known as still life, from several viewpoints at once. After a journalist said that one of Braque's paintings looked like "bizarre cubes," the style came to be called Cubism. Because all the different angles often looked confusing, in 1912, Picasso and Braque began adding collage materials to their paintings, to give clues about what they were.

When World War I broke out in 1914, as Picasso was Spanish, he was allowed to stay in Paris while most of his French friends had to go and fight.

During the war, a new ballet was created in Paris for the Ballets Russes. *Parade* was first performed there in 1917. Inspired by Cubism, Picasso designed the costumes, stage sets, and curtain, using vivid colors and angled shapes. He also made new friends, including a dancer, Olga Khokhlova, who became his first wife.

Picasso's son Paulo was born in 1921, and after taking a holiday with Olga and Paulo, Picasso began painting large, heavy-looking bathers. Then he became involved with the new Surrealist movement, which explored dreams and the subconscious mind. Some call this his Monster period.

Picasso created more sets for the Ballets Russes and began making metal sculptures as well as painting and printmaking. In 1927, he met a young lady named Marie-Thérèse Walter who became the subject of many of his new style of curving, flat-looking paintings with distorted shapes, continuing some of his

Cubist ideas. In 1930, while in Switzerland, he bought an Airedale terrier and named him Elft. Five years later, he split up with Olga and took Elft to live with Marie-Thérèse and their new baby daughter, Maya.

The **Minotaur**, a creature that had a bull's head and tail on a man's body, was written about in ancient myths. Minotaurs appeared in many of Picasso's works, including an etching he called *Minotauromachy*, showing a Minotaur invading a sculptor's studio.

Starting in 1931, violent social and political unrest occurred in Spain. In July 1936, the Spanish Civil War began when the Spanish army rebelled against the elected Republican government. Although he lived in France, Picasso was extremely worried and upset about his home country. That year, he also met a photographer, Dora Maar.

In 1937, the Spanish Republican government asked Picasso to create a mural for Spain's pavilion at a big Paris exhibition. Then in April, news broke of a bombing raid on the defenseless Spanish town of Guernica. Picasso painted a massive black and white mural representing the violence in Guernica. It was not the glorious image the government had wanted. Picasso also painted *Weeping Woman* using Dora as his model. It was another image about the horrors of Guernica and the Spanish Civil War.

In 1937, Picasso bought an Afghan greyhound that he named Kazbek. In Paris during World War II, he met a young painter named Françoise Gilot. He also began making sculptures from things he found lying around, such as a bicycle saddle and a child's toy car. He and Françoise had two children, Claude and Paloma. They also had a pet dog, Yan the boxer. In 1953, he began living with his new partner, Jacqueline Roque, who became his second wife, in the South of France with Yan, their pet goat Esmeralda, and a dalmatian named Perro. In 1957, a friend visited Picasso with his dachshund, Lump. Lump never left, and he and Picasso became inseparable. Lump was pampered, and Picasso often painted him, creating original styles of art until the end of his life.

Lump

FRiDA KaHLO

FROM MEXiCO with PASSiON

This iconic and celebrated artist loved the company of animals, and many of them made it into her powerful paintings. Spider monkeys, a hairless dog, parakeets, macaws, and even a fawn were Kahlo's true loves.

Born in 1907 in Mexico, Magdalena Carmen Frida Kahlo y Calderón later shortened her name to Frida Kahlo. She grew up with her parents and six sisters. Even though Frida always loved animals the family didn't have any pets when she was little. When she was three, the Mexican Revolution began. It was a bitter and violent struggle that lasted 10 years and changed Frida's life and the way the country was run.

When Frida was six, she caught a disease called polio, which damaged her right leg. From then on, she always covered up her leg with her clothing, but still, other children cruelly nicknamed her "Peg-leg Frida."

At 18, Kahlo hoped to become a doctor. She lived in a small village called Coyoacán, inside Mexico City and about an hour's bus ride from her school. One day, as the bus driver turned a corner, he collided with a cable car. Kahlo's lower body was crushed in the accident, causing terrible injuries that affected her for the rest of her life. In enormous pain, she had to lie in a body cast for three months, and she spent the rest of her life in and out of hospitals, having 35 operations. She could not have children and was never without pain.

Soon after the accident, Kahlo's mom had a special easel made for her that she could use in bed, and her father gave her some paints. They thought it would cheer her up. Kahlo taught herself to paint.

Kahlo's paintings expressed her feelings and pain. Eventually, she learned to walk again, and she decided she wanted to be an artist.

Starting in the 1920s, the Mexican government paid for certain artists to paint murals on the walls of public buildings, such as churches, schools, and libraries, to show the country's history and to help bring everyone back together after the revolution. There were three main Mexican mural painters: José Clemente Orozco, David Alfaro Siqueiros, and Diego Rivera, who later became Kahlo's husband.

Kahlo first met Diego Rivera when she was a student, asking for advice on her art career. They fell in love and married in 1929. Kahlo was Rivera's third wife. He was 42 and large; she was 22 and tiny. Her parents referred to them as "the elephant and the dove."

Kahlo and Rivera had an extremely stormy marriage. He was rarely faithful, and they separated several times. Although she spent a lot of time in the hospital, over her career, she painted 143 paintings, 55 of them self-portraits. These show her suffering and loneliness but also how determined she was; she painted many paintings in bed. She even had a mirror placed over her bed so she could paint self-portraits.

Kahlo kept many pets, which she loved passionately. Almost a substitute for the children she could not have, she featured them in many paintings. They included two or three spider monkeys, one named Fulang Chang, a gift from Rivera, and another named Caimito de Guayabal; several Mexican hairless dogs (Xoloitzcuintli) including her favorite, Sr. Xolotl; parrots, including Bonito, an Amazon breed who performed tricks for pats of butter; parakeets; macaws; chickens; sparrows; an eagle named Gertrudis Caca Blanca; and a dainty fawn named Granizo.

The name of Kahlo's favorite dog breed, **Xoloitzcuintli**, comes from Nahuatl, the language spoken by the Aztecs. Composed of two names, *xolotl*, meaning "god," and *itzcuintli*, meaning "dog," it translates as "God's dog."

Kahlo frequently used symbols in her paintings to tell underlying stories, and many of her animals represent different meanings. For instance, her monkeys symbolize either protection or evil, a hummingbird stands for good luck or the end of her marriage, a black cat means bad luck or death, and her deer suggests being hunted.

Her home was called Casa Azul, or "Blue House" in Spanish. In the garden, Rivera built a pyramid structure for some of the animals to sleep in. Also in the garden, Kahlo planted colorful, tropical plants and arranged Mexican sculptures. Extremely proud of her heritage, she also wore traditional Mexican costumes and hairstyles.

In 1931, in San Francisco County Hospital, Kahlo met Dr. Leo Eloesser, a well-known bone surgeon and a friend of Rivera's. He became her doctor for the rest of her life. The following year, she and Rivera moved to the United States as Rivera had been commissioned to paint a mural at the Detroit Institute of Arts. They also lived in Philadelphia and New York and stayed in the US for almost three years. Rivera loved the United States, but Kahlo missed Mexico. When they returned, she had more operations.

Kahlo once said, "I paint myself because I'm so often alone and because I am the subject I know best." Simplified and brightly colored, her paintings are often described as folk art. In 1937, four of her paintings were shown for the first time in public in a Mexican exhibition.

In 1938, the French poet and Surrealist André Breton visited Mexico. When he saw Kahlo's work, he said she was a Surrealist. Surrealists made art about dreams and people's unconscious thoughts. Although Kahlo said she was not a Surrealist, she accepted his offer to show her work in Paris. Later that year, she traveled to New York for her first solo exhibition, and the following year, she went to Paris for the Mexique exhibition of her work. One of the paintings shown was a self-portrait that became the first work by a 20th-century Mexican artist to be bought by the famous Louvre museum in Paris. That November, she and Rivera were divorced.

In 1940, early in World War II, Breton organized the International Surrealist Exhibition at the Gallery of Mexican Art in Mexico City. Kahlo and Rivera took part, although they did not consider themselves Surrealists. That December, she and Rivera remarried.

Because her themes are sometimes bizarre and disturbing, Kahlo is often called a Surrealist, but unlike the Surrealists who explored dreams and the subconscious, Kahlo painted images about her real life. It was not until 1953 that her first solo exhibition was held in Mexico. By then, she was extremely ill. Dr. Eloesser said she was not well enough to attend the opening, but she was determined. She arranged for her bed to be delivered to the gallery while she followed in an ambulance. She was carried to her bed and greeted everyone at the exhibition.

Soon after, however, Kahlo's badly infected right leg had to be amputated below the knee. The following year, she became particularly ill and was mainly bed-ridden. In July 1954, she died at home in Casa Azul. She was 47 years old.

Norman Rockwell

American Illustrator

America's most famous illustrator,
Norman Rockwell painted 20th-century
American life for nearly 70 years,
featuring many different people
and his own pets and friends' dogs.

Born in New York City in 1894, Norman Rockwell wanted to be an artist since he was a kid. At 14, he began art classes at the New York School of Art and later studied at the National Academy of Design and the Art Students League.

As a student, Rockwell worked in all sorts of part-time jobs, but by the time he was 18, he was earning enough from his art to live on. While he was still at the Art Students League, he was commissioned by a neighbor to paint four Christmas cards, and soon after, he was illustrating his first book. He was employed as an illustrator for the Boy Scouts' magazine, *Boys' Life*. It was his first regular job as an illustrator, and he stayed there for three years. In 1920, he painted a picture for the Boy Scouts calendar and it was so popular that for the next 50 years he painted an illustration for each calendar.

For some time, Rockwell had wanted to paint cover pictures for the *Saturday Evening Post*, as its cover illustrations were admired throughout the United States. When he was 22, with no appointment, he took a train to the magazine's headquarters in Philadelphia and showed the editor two paintings and three sketched ideas.

As soon as he saw them, the editor of the magazine bought Rockwell's illustrations and asked him to turn the sketches into paintings. The first of these that appeared on the cover, in May 1916, was *Mother's Day Off,* or *Boy with Baby Carriage.* It shows three boys, one dressed as a grown man, pushing his baby sister in her pram, and two in casual clothes, teasing him. Billy Paine was the cheeky young boy who posed for all three boys in the picture, and he became one of Rockwell's favorite models.

From their first meeting, Rockwell and George Horace Lorimer, the editor of the *Post*, got on well.

Lorimer saw Rockwell's huge talent immediately. He could draw and paint and capture human characteristics and personality. He could also show his love and understanding of dogs' characters and behavior.

Dogs were important to Rockwell in his art and in real life. He often put them in prominent places in illustrations, for their boldness and appeal. His own dogs went with him to his studio and dozed on the floor as he worked. He also borrowed neighbors' dogs to model, and he often included other animals, including chickens, horses, cows, and even deer and a bear.

In a folder, Rockwell kept hundreds of photographs and magazine clippings of dogs to use as references  for his pictures. He preferred mongrels, or dogs of no definable type of breed, so he labeled the folder "**Mutts**."

Rockwell advised that any artists painting animals should draw and paint them "just as carefully and understandingly as you paint the people." Over his life, he had several pet dogs who kept him company in his studio, including dogs named Pitter, Butch, Beagle, and Lassie.

In the year that his first illustration appeared on the cover of the *Saturday Evening Post*, Rockwell married Irene O'Conner. Their marriage lasted from 1916 to 1929.

During World War I, Rockwell applied to join the US Navy but they would not let him in as he was eight pounds underweight. That evening, he filled himself up with lots of food and drink, including bananas and doughnuts, and the next day he reapplied and they allowed him in, but only as a military artist, not in a fighting position.

Over the years, Rockwell's covers became well known and popular, and they even became collector's items. In 1927, Charles Lindbergh made the first solo flight across the Atlantic, inspiring the whole of America, and Rockwell created a cover to celebrate the event. For decades, his paintings captured the hearts of Americans and helped to raise the *Saturday Evening Post* to the status of "America's magazine," with over six million subscribers at one point.

Rockwell developed his pictures in a series of carefully planned steps. First, he drew a loose sketch of his idea. Next, he gathered together his models, costumes, and props and researched the background. Then, he made individual drawings of each part of the picture in great detail, after which he made color sketches. Finally, he drew and painted his final illustration.

During the 1920s, Rockwell became rich and famous. He produced a cover illustration for the *Saturday Evening Post* nearly every month, and his salary was doubled. From 1919 to 1943, he created the covers for every Christmas edition of the *Post*. He also worked for other magazines, including the *Literary Digest*, *Country Gentleman*, *Leslie's Weekly*, *Judge*, *People's Popular Monthly*, and *Life*.

The 1930s and 1940s were extremely busy. In 1930, three weeks after they met, he married his second wife, Mary Barstow. They had three sons: Jarvis, Thomas, and Peter. In 1939, just before the

outbreak of World War II in Europe, they moved
to Vermont from New York. Different sights and
scenery gave him creative new ideas. In 1943, he
painted the Four Freedoms series, which became
iconic works of art. He completed all four paintings
in seven months and lost 15 pounds in weight.

The Four Freedoms series was inspired by President Franklin D. Roosevelt's speech describing universal rights: *Freedom from Want*, *Freedom of Speech*, *Freedom of Worship*, and *Freedom from Fear*. After appearing on the *Post* covers, the paintings toured America and raised millions of dollars for the war effort.

In 1953, the Rockwells moved to Massachusetts, but in 1959, Mary died suddenly from a heart attack. Two years later, Rockwell married his third wife, Molly Punderson, who encouraged him to move on from the *Post* to make covers for *Look* magazine instead. His last of 361 covers for the *Post* was published in 1963. Rather than family issues, his new illustrations highlighted social issues, including civil rights, poverty, and space exploration. In 1977, he was awarded the Presidential Medal of Freedom by President Ford. Over his career, Rockwell created more than 4,000 paintings for books, magazines, and all sorts of publications. He died in 1978, aged 84.

GUSTAV KLIMT

GOLDEN MAN OF
ART NOUVEAU

This famous Austrian Art Nouveau painter had a passion for beautiful art and women, but most of all for cats. His studio was always full of pet felines—and the beautiful models he painted.

Gustav Klimt was born in Vienna, Austria, in 1862. While at school, he and his younger brothers, Ernst and Georg, excelled at art. Although he loved animals all his life, Gustav's family was poor so they could not afford pets. He made up for that when he was grown up.

As a teenager, Gustav attended the Viennese School of Applied Art. His teachers noticed his extraordinary talent and selected him to take extra art classes. Soon, his brothers joined him there, along with their friend Franz Matsch. While they were still studying, Gustav, Ernst, and Franz were chosen to paint pictures for money. In 1879, when Gustav was 17, they created designs for Festzug, a pageant organized for the whole of Vienna to celebrate the silver wedding anniversary of their emperor and empress. Artist Hans Makart was in charge of the project.

Hans Makart was one of the greatest Viennese painters at the time. Because he painted huge canvases with intense colors, he was nicknamed the "magician of color" and the "prince of painters."

Klimt learned from his ideas about using color to create light effects.

Gustav, Ernst, and Franz were asked to paint large murals on the walls and ceilings of public and private buildings, including Empress Elisabeth's country house; the grand Burgtheater, the Austrian national theater; and the Kunsthistorisches Museum. Klimt was also asked to illustrate some books.

The three successful young artists called themselves the Künstler-Compagnie (Artists' Company), and they worked in a studio near the center of Vienna. In 1888, the emperor awarded them the Goldene Verdienstkreuz, or the Golden Order of Merit, for their outstanding work, which was a great honor.

Across Vienna, Klimt had become famous. But then tragedy struck. First his father died at 58 and then his brother Ernst also died at just 28. Heartbroken, Klimt began supporting his mother, four sisters, and Ernst's young wife and baby daughter through working as an artist. For most of his life, Klimt lived with his mother and sisters. He felt particularly comfortable in the company of females and cats. He had many female friends—and pet cats—but he never married.

Soon after Ernst died, Klimt became friends with a young lady named Emilie Flöge. Flöge and her sisters owned the most well-known dressmaker's shop in Vienna, and they often modeled for Klimt, sometimes wearing the dresses they made and sometimes wearing more expensive fashions from London. Klimt and Flöge went to the opera and took French lessons together.

Although Klimt had achieved fame early in his career, he was not satisfied. He wanted to create new, modern art, not follow old traditions. The Vienna Künstlerhaus (Artists' House) was a powerful organization that controlled most of the art that was made and exhibited in Vienna, but Klimt thought it was old-fashioned and had too much control over the art that was made in the city. In 1897, he and some other artists set up a new, independent association: the Vienna Secession. The artists elected Klimt to be their first president.

The Vienna Secessionists built their own exhibition building, held their own exhibitions, and produced their own magazine, *Ver Sacrum* ("Sacred Spring"), because they said that their art was like fresh new plant shoots of spring. Although Klimt preferred painting to writing, he wrote several articles for *Ver Sacrum*.

From the start of the Vienna Secession, Klimt painted in an entirely new style. He loved to paint people, especially strong women. His painting *Pallas Athene* was the first of these. In bright colors, he included flowers, swirls, and other patterns. These decorative elements were often in the background, while the women looked soft and realistic. Usually at that time, other artists depicted women as delicate, but Klimt's were strong because he understood women. He liked his models to relax as they posed in his studio, and most did because Klimt let his pet cats wander around freely. The models happily stroked the cats as they padded around, walking all over Klimt's drawings. Klimt always had several pet cats, and not just two or three—sometimes he had about 10.

From 1899 to 1910, Klimt worked in his Golden Phase. As well as using dyed paint, he also painted with gold and silver and decorated his pictures even more. He developed this completely new style of art through studying Japanese art and ancient Byzantine mosaics he saw in Venice.

In 1902, using colorful
paint, gold and silver,
fragments of semiprecious materials,
and other odds and ends including nails, buttons,
tin tacks, and pieces of mirror and dyed glass,
Klimt created his huge *Beethoven Frieze*, a seven-
part painting to celebrate the life of the composer
Ludwig van Beethoven. Creating a powerful
impact, Klimt used symbolism to suggest that art
and love will rescue the human race from greed
and dishonesty. Although most people loved the
work, some did not understand his meaning.

In 1903, the magazine *Ver Sacrum* stopped
publication, and also the 18th Secessionist Exhibition
was held, devoted to Klimt. For the first time, he

exhibited some of his landscape paintings as well as portraits, including those of Gertha Felsövanyi and Emilie Flöge, which were painted in his new style of a single woman wearing an elaborate outfit, set against a plain background decorated with gold. Only their hands and faces are painted realistically.

In 1904, an architect friend of Klimt built a mansion called the Stoclet Palace in Brussels. Klimt decorated three walls of the dining room with an exotic mosaic. Using expensive materials, including enamel, glass, ceramics, metals, coral, mother-of-pearl, and semiprecious jewels, these mosaics came to be called the *Stoclet Frieze*. Like his other paintings, the frieze is also full of symbols.

Katze

It is not clear whether or not Klimt called many of his cats "**Katze**," which simply means "cat" in German, or just one of his beloved black and white cats that he was photographed cuddling.

In 1905, Klimt and some others broke away from the Vienna Secession over disagreements about art. Instead, they formed the Klimt Group.

In 1908, Klimt exhibited several paintings, including *The Kiss*. With its gold and silver leaf, brilliant colors, symbolism, and graceful curves, it is Klimt's most famous work, featuring  a man and woman entwined, wrapped in golden patterned clothes and standing on a patch of flowers. In the painting, the man leans over the woman to kiss her.

In February 1918, near the end of World War I, Klimt died from pneumonia and influenza. He was 55. By time, his decorative style of art had become old-fashioned, but a few years later, it became one of the most admired aspects of Art Nouveau.

PAUL KLEE

CREATIVE WIT

A unique and original Swiss-German artist, Paul Klee loved music, color… and cats. He said drawing was "taking a line for a walk."

Although born in Switzerland, Paul Klee (pronounced "clay") inherited his father's German citizenship. His dad was a music teacher and his mom a singer. Both Paul and his older sister, Mathilde, learned to play musical instruments; Klee began playing the violin when he was seven. He loved animals and grew up with pet cats, carrying on when he was an adult.

As a young child, Paul was taught to draw by his grandmother, and his music teacher talked to him about music and art history. He was an outstanding violinist, but he chose to become an artist rather than a musician. By then—the end of the 19th century—creative ideas were especially encouraged in Munich, Germany, and in 1898, he enrolled at the Academy of Fine Arts there and had lessons with the artist and architect Franz von Stuck.

Although Klee was good at drawing, he felt he did not understand color and so could not paint. We know what he thought because from 1897 to 1918, he wrote his thoughts in diaries. But he finished his fine art degree in 1901 and traveled around Italy for six months with a friend, studying the great artists of the past. After returning from Italy to Bern, Switzerland, he lived again with his parents for four years.

Klee had met Lily Stumpf, a pianist, in 1899. They had much in common; both loved music, art, and cats. They became engaged, but they did not announce it because Klee did not earn enough from his art and Stumpf's father disapproved of the match, so he would not let them marry.

By 1905, Klee was experimenting with all kinds of art techniques and starting to exhibit his works. He was trying to earn money through art, violin playing, and writing concert and theater reviews.

That year, he stayed in Paris for two weeks with friends. In his diary, he wrote of his enthusiasm for the art he saw in Paris, especially the paintings of the Impressionists. The Impressionists painted with bright colors and small marks, capturing the effects of light. Back in Switzerland, he discovered the art of Edvard Munch and James Ensor. His head was buzzing with ideas for creating art.

In September 1906, Klee and Lily Stumpf married and settled in Munich. They started their married life with Lily giving piano lessons and Paul keeping house and painting. They held musical evenings for friends. In November 1907, their son Felix Paul was born.

Klee shared his studio with his pet cats, especially one beautiful, white, long-haired cat named Bimbo, who followed him everywhere.

Bimbo

But Klee was devoted to every cat he had.
One was a tabby named Fritzi. Then there
was Bimbo, and then another cat named
Bimbo II. Mys was a dark, long-haired cat.
He had another long-haired cat named
Nuggi and another tabby named Skunk.
He never minded his cats walking across
his wet paintings as he said that in years to
come, people would wonder how he created
the effects! His cats inspired him, and he
produced nearly 30 works with cats
in them.

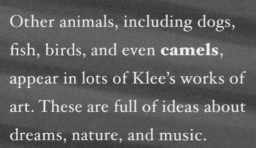

Other animals, including dogs,
fish, birds, and even **camels**,
appear in lots of Klee's works of
art. These are full of ideas about
dreams, nature, and music.

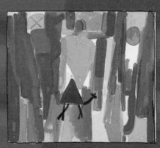

In 1907, Klee was inspired by the French Post-Impressionists, especially Henri de Toulouse-Lautrec and Vincent van Gogh. In 1910, he had his first solo exhibition around Switzerland. In 1911, he met the artists Wassily Kandinsky and Franz Marc, who formed Der Blaue Reiter (the Blue Rider), a group that expressed emotions through paintings. The three artists shared a love of animals and music, and they became close friends. Klee's art was influenced by several new art movements: Expressionism, art about feelings; Cubism, pictures painted from several angles at once; and Surrealism, art about subconscious thoughts and dreams. Klee's art was also often light-hearted and childlike because he felt that children—like animals—were open and trustworthy. In Paris in 1912, he met Robert Delaunay, an artist who put certain colors next to each other to make them appear brighter.

In 1914, Klee visited Tunisia. Excited by the quality of light there, he wrote, "Color has taken possession of me; no longer do I have to chase after it, I know that it has hold of me forever...color and I are one. I am a painter." He meant that he had discovered how to use color and so believed he could paint, and from then, he painted vibrant works in many different styles.

Before every painting session, Klee warmed up by playing his violin. He was outstanding at drawing, and his harmonious paintings also show his understanding of music and rhythm.

Three months after Klee returned from Tunisia, World War I began. Two years later, as a German citizen, he was enlisted into the army. His job was to paint aircraft.

In 1918, Klee left the army and returned home to Lily and Felix and their cats. He continued to paint and experiment, developing new printing and painting techniques. By this time, he had become well known and was earning good money from his art.

In 1919, an architect named Walter Gropius started a new art school in Germany. Called the Bauhaus, it taught students all the arts, including design and crafts, and how to produce their art and designs to earn money. It was revolutionary, and Klee and his friend Kandinsky were among the first artists to teach there. Klee instructed his students about composition (the overall arrangement) and color. By now he had become an expert in scientific color theories, so he knew how to make colors look extra vibrant in paintings. One of his friends wrote in a book about Klee's love for animals, especially cats. "Paul Klee adores cats," she wrote. "In Dessau, his cat always looked out the window in the studio.

 I could see him perfectly from my private room. Klee told me the cat looked at me insistently: You can't have any secrets. My cat will tell me all." The cat on the windowsill was, of course, Bimbo, who also appears in

Marina Alberghini's book, expressively titled *Il gatto cosmico di Paul Klee* ("Paul Klee's Cosmic Cat").

Many of Klee's paintings are made up of brightly colored shapes, inspired by his spiritual beliefs. Some paintings are just colored squares, which one art historian called his "magic squares." With its many influences, Klee's work challenged traditional art. He often used his own made-up symbols and signs that he developed from letters, musical notes, or children's drawings. In many ways, his paintings are like cheery, painted tunes. After visiting Egypt in 1928, his paintings became even more colorful and mystical. That year he painted *Cat and Bird*, one of several paintings that show his love of cats. A cat's face with a bird painted on its forehead, it symbolizes what the cat is thinking. The bird is the cat's secret desire, shown also by the heart-shaped nose.

Klee died in 1940, having produced almost 10,000 works over his lifetime.

Suzanne Valadon

French Artist
& Model

Cats must have seen similarities to themselves in this bold, independent, smart, and beautiful artist—as several followed her home, where she fed and cared for them. Her artist son adored cats as much as she did.

Marie Clémentine Valadon was born in a small town in northeastern France. She and her mother were poor, and they moved to Montmartre in Paris when she was five. By the time she was 11, she had to work to earn money. She loved cats but was too poor to have one. Montmartre was a poor but bustling area, and Marie had several jobs: pastry cook, vegetable seller, waitress, and circus acrobat. At 15, however, she fell from a trapeze, hurting her back and ending her circus career.

As Montmartre was a lively artists' community, Marie became an artists' model. For over 10 years, she modeled for several artists, including Pierre Puvis de Chavannes, Berthe Morisot, Pierre-Auguste Renoir, and Henri de Toulouse-Lautrec. Although her name was Marie, Toulouse-Lautrec nicknamed her Suzanne after a biblical character, and she preferred it.

Inspired by the community around her, in between modeling, Valadon began drawing and painting. She produced colorful drawings and still lifes, portraits, and flower and landscape paintings. She also painted female nudes, which in those days was a highly unusual subject for women artists.

Artists loved painting Valadon, as she was dark haired and attractive, and she stood or sat still! Renoir, a well-known Impressionist, painted her in several famous pictures, including *Dance at Bougival*, *City Dance*, *Girl Braiding Her Hair*, and *Suzanne Valadon*. When she was 18, she had a son she named Maurice Utrillo, although many people did not believe that one of her boyfriends, Spanish artist Miguel Utrillo, was actually Maurice's father. If he was not, however, no one ever knew who Maurice's father really was.

In the early 1890s, Valadon became friends with the artist Edgar Degas, who was not known as a friendly person. Yet Degas and Valadon became close. Degas encouraged Valadon with her art and bought some of her drawings and paintings. They remained close friends until his death in 1917.

At first, Valadon drew more than painted, but from 1892, she painted more. That year, she painted her first female nude. Also during the 1890s, she exhibited her work, often at the Galerie Bernheim-Jeune in Paris, and initially she mostly exhibited portraits. Her first models were Maurice, her mother, her niece, and the composer and pianist Erik Satie, who was her boyfriend for six months in 1893. In 1896, she married the banker Paul Moussis, and for the first time, she could afford to become a full-time painter.

For a lot of the time, Maurice was looked after by both Suzanne and her mother. As he grew up, Maurice became difficult. He often missed school, and when he was older, he became an alcoholic. At 21, he suffered with a mental illness, and to help him, Valadon encouraged him to paint. She taught him what Degas had taught her, and to her delight, he had great artistic skills and was soon drawing and painting around Montmartre.

Over the years, Valadon had many cats that she loved dearly. Every Friday, rather than cat food, she gave them expensive beluga caviar. Maurice loved cats as much as his mother did.

For several years, besides her cats, Suzanne Valadon also had a German sheepdog and a **goat**. She fed the goat her drawings if she was not happy with them.

By 1910, Maurice had become famous for his paintings of Montmartre. By then, Valadon was exhibiting her paintings at the Paris Salon, an important annual exhibition where a jury selected the art to be displayed. Some of her paintings that were displayed at the Salon included *Adam and Eve*, *The Joy of Living*, and *Casting of the Net*.

Mainly using oil paint, oil pencils, pastels, and red chalk, Valadon created richly colored pictures and often outlined objects and figures with black lines to show their curves and structure.

Her intense colors were inspired by her friends who were Post-Impressionists and by the Fauvist art movement. Post-Impressionists were among the first artists to paint with bold, bright colors to express the way they felt about the scenes they painted. The Fauves came after them and painted in even bolder colors, distorting their views of nature. Valadon was not shy about painting strong or nude women, which contrasted with the usual depictions of passive females. This probably reflected her own personal outlook on life.

Before Valadon married Moussis, she had affairs with several of the artists she modeled for, including Puvis de Chavannes and Renoir. For 14 years, she remained married to Moussis, but when she was 44, she met the artist André Utter, who was 23. She left her husband for him. They had several joint exhibitions, and Utter posed for some of her paintings.

Valadon's cats were also often her models. She painted several during her career: tabby cats, white cats, and ginger, or orange, cats. In the paintings, they sit or relax on tables, rugs, or blankets; near flowers; or on the laps of Valadon's friends. She rarely named her cats in her paintings, except for one.

In 1919, she found Raminou in
a Montmartre alleyway. She painted
him several times, and like the other
cats in her paintings, he always looks
contented and well fed.

Valadon was unusual during a time when most
women conformed to a certain way of behaving.
Bold and confident, she was friends with men and
women, was outspoken and determined to make
her way as an artist, and did not give up working
as most women did after marriage. Many described
her as beautiful and voluptuous, with blue eyes,
porcelain skin, and thick, dark hair "the color of
cognac."

Utter and Valadon married when World War I
began in 1914, and Utter volunteered for military
service. As a soldier's wife, she received an allow-
ance from the army. Maurice, on the other hand,
was rejected for military service and was once
again sent to a mental institution. Valadon painted

little during that time, although she had her first solo exhibition in 1915.

Valadon's first solo exhibition in 1915 was a great success. Although many visitors were shocked by her paintings, some other artists and art critics admired them. She became the first female painter to be accepted into the prestigious Société Nationale des Beaux-Arts, making her extremely successful at a time when few women became artists.

After the war, Valadon carried on painting and drawing, and in 1920, she was elected to exhibit in the prestigious Salon d'Automne. In 1924, she signed a contract with the Bernheim-Jeune art gallery, which gave her an income. She bought a country estate, but by the 1930s her health began to decline. Maurice and Utter moved out, but she was never lonely; the rest of her life was filled with friends and cats.

Ai WEiWEi

Chinese Philosopher
& Artist

One of the world's most influential and talked-about contemporary artists, Ai Weiwei lives with about 40 cats in his Beijing studio home. He treats them with great respect—and they choose him, not the other way around.

The most famous contemporary Chinese artist,
Ai Weiwei lives with lots of cats. He is also a human
rights activist, and because of this, he has been
arrested in China and put under surveillance
(watched by the authorities). Meanwhile, he
continues to make a wide variety of art, combining
his belief in helping others with his love of art.
His creations range from huge installations and
architectural projects to small constructions,
photographs, and videos.

Ai was born in Beijing in 1957. His father, Ai Qing,
was one of China's most important modern poets.
At 21, Ai went to the Beijing Film Academy and

studied animation. Three years later, he moved to New York so he could attend the famous Parsons School of Design. In 1985, he went to the Art Students League of New York for three years.

When he finished studying, Ai stayed in New York City and earned money by working odd jobs and drawing portraits. In between, he created art out of ready-made objects. Everywhere he went, he carried a camera and took photos, recording all he saw. He also became fascinated by blackjack card games and casinos. In 1993, he returned to China because his dad was ill.

With his great energy, Ai carried on doing many different things. First, he helped to establish an artists' group called Beijing East Village. Then, in 1994, 1995, and 1997, he and a friend published three books about the artists in the group. In 1999, he built himself a studio house in the northeast of Beijing. Four years later, he started an architecture studio called FAKE Design.

In honor of his dad, Ai created the Ai Qing Memorial in Jinhua Ai Qing Cultural Park, Jinhua, Zhejiang, in 2003. In 2005, he was asked to write a blog, which he wrote each day for four years, expressing many thoughts, including criticisms of his government, ideas about art and architecture, and stories about his life.

In May 2008, a huge earthquake hit the Sichuan province in southwest China. Thousands of people died. Ai led a team to film where the earthquake had happened. Through an investigation, he found out the names of all the children who had died in the disaster. He believed that cheap materials and poor construction methods had been used to build schools and other buildings, which was why they collapsed in the earthquake and so many had died. He made an art installation out of his findings, including lists of all the children's names that had died and a massive, curving sculpture made of 90 tons of bent and twisted rebar—the metal used to reinforce buildings. Ai collected and straightened it all by hand, creating a monument to the victims. He was imprisoned for 81 days by the Chinese authorities in 2011 because of this.

Ai's art often mixes Chinese culture and heritage with the art and culture that he experienced in America, and he uses this to comment on how we all live, standing up for those who are oppressed or leading difficult lives. To do this, he boldly crosses many boundaries and accepted art ideas. He says that the 20th-century French artist Marcel Duchamp and German artist Joseph Beuys are his biggest influences. Like Ai, these artists challenged conventions in life and art.

Ai is one of the first famous artists to use social media such as Instagram and Twitter. Yet he also emphasizes traditional Chinese crafts. In some works, he has considered how the industrial world has made craft less important, such as in *Colored Vases* of 2009–10. An expert in ancient Chinese ceramics, he collected several priceless Han dynasty pots and painted them in vivid colors, which was shocking in itself. Then he was filmed smashing them. This showed his opinion that machine-made objects are replacing valuable craft-made items that were created with precision and skill. Another of his works was an installation at Tate Modern in London, called *Sunflower Seeds*, in 2010. Approximately 1,600 Chinese craft workers made 100 million hand-painted porcelain sunflower seeds, which were poured on to the floor. The porcelain seeds represented the Chinese people.

For some time, Ai was watched by the authorities and had to work in a building with cameras on him all day. To keep him company, he encouraged local cats to join him and, recognizing his kindness and compassion, many soon made themselves at home around him. He has always loved cats, and now

he shares the studio he designed for himself in Beijing with more than 40 of them, plus several dogs. He also often posts pictures of the animals on Instagram. In 2006, in one of his blog entries, he wrote, "The cats and dogs in my home enjoy a high status, they seem more like the lords of the manor than I do."

Ai respects and loves all the cats and dogs that live with him and gives them as much freedom as he can. It gives him great happiness to make them feel safe and comfortable. Ai makes sure they are well fed, and he is affectionate with all of them. They are allowed to wander around his work, and they give him great pleasure. He explained, "The poses they strike in the courtyard often inspire more joy in me than the house itself. Their self-important

In a 2012 documentary, *Ai Weiwei: Never Sorry*, Ai told how one of his cats had learned to **open doors**.

positions seem to be saying, 'This is my territory,' and that makes me happy. However, I've never designed a special place for them. I can't think like an animal, which is part of the reason I respect them; it's impossible for me to enter into their realm."

All of Ai's art develops from what he sees in the world around him mixed with his understanding of human nature. Much of it is precisely and carefully designed and produced, often using traditional, expert craft methods and a wide range of materials. As well as being an artist, he has worked as a card player, filmmaker, photographer, writer, painter, publisher, curator, architect, and blogger.

He has had large solo exhibitions of his art in America, Britain, Taiwan, and Germany, and he has been involved with important architectural projects, including helping to design the 2008 Olympic stadium in Beijing and the 2012 Serpentine Galleries Pavilion in London. He has won several prestigious prizes, including a lifetime achievement award from the Chinese Contemporary Art Awards in 2008 and Amnesty International's Ambassador of Conscience Award in 2015.

ROMARE BEARDEN

POWERFUL
VISUAL VOICE

American artist Romare Bearden's dazzling collages, paintings, cartoons, books, and articles expressed black American life in the mid-20th century, but his cats cared more for his cuddles.

Born in North Carolina, Romare Bearden was the only child in a middle-class African American family. When Romare was three, the Beardens moved to New York City. Many African Americans were moving north at the time because of racial struggles in the South. This mass movement of so many people was called the Great Migration. The Beardens settled in Harlem, a vibrant neighborhood in Manhattan, where Romare's parents actively supported their local community.

Romare Bearden's art featured memories of his childhood, growing up having **roosters** and **cats**.

By 1918, many people involved in the Harlem
Renaissance met at the Bearden house. The
Harlem Renaissance was a cultural, social, and
artistic development that came to be seen as
a rebirth of African American arts.

In the 1920s, the Beardens moved to Pittsburgh,
and when he left school, Romare (his friends called
him Romie) played semiprofessional baseball.

Bearden went to three universities: Lincoln
University, Boston University, and New York
University (NYU). He studied mathematics,
science, and education, and while at NYU, he
became interested in art, particularly cartoons.
Although his degree was in education, he decided
he wanted to be a cartoonist. So while at NYU, he
took some art courses at the Art Students League,
which had first opened in New York City in 1875.
With its informal approach of no grading or degree
programs, it attracted both amateur and professional
artists. Bearden was taught by several artist-teachers,

including the expressive German artist George Grosz. While still studying, Bearden exhibited some of his paintings at the Harlem YMCA and the Harlem Art Workshop. They were brightly colored and simplified. Bearden supported himself through college working as an art editor and also drawing cartoons for several African American newspapers.

George Grosz was known for his drawings and paintings that depicted his view of life in Berlin, and he gave Bearden his first real art training, encouraging him to study Old Master painters and the art movements that were happening around that time. Bearden became especially interested in Post-Impressionism, Cubism, and Futurism, and also in the collages that Grosz created.

During that time, Bearden joined 74 other black artists to establish the Harlem Artists Guild. They met socially and discussed the politics of the day, including subjects that were particularly affecting them, including racism, poverty, and unemployment —and their art. Using both watercolor and oil paints, Bearden began creating art influenced by his experiences of living in different parts of America, especially with images of the American South.

In 1940, Bearden had his first one-man exhibition in Harlem, surprising visitors with his colorful, bold paintings. But World War II had broken out in Europe, and soon Bearden was enlisted in the US Army. From 1942 to 1945, he served as an army sergeant in the 372nd Infantry Regiment. After the war, he continued producing oil paintings and watercolors, but as he did not earn enough from his art, he also worked as a case worker for the New York City Department of Social Services, a job he kept until 1969. In 1945, he had two more successful solo shows, in Washington, DC, and New York City. By that time, his art had changed, expressing his feelings about the lack of compassion he had seen in the world during the war, often through religious subject matter.

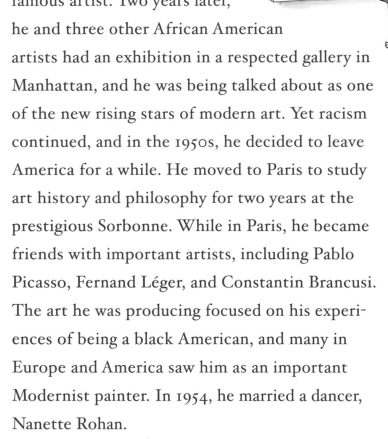

Bearden's New York exhibition in 1945 was a great success, and the Museum of Modern Art (MoMA) bought one of his paintings. This was a hugely important step in becoming a famous artist. Two years later, he and three other African American artists had an exhibition in a respected gallery in Manhattan, and he was being talked about as one of the new rising stars of modern art. Yet racism continued, and in the 1950s, he decided to leave America for a while. He moved to Paris to study art history and philosophy for two years at the prestigious Sorbonne. While in Paris, he became friends with important artists, including Pablo Picasso, Fernand Léger, and Constantin Brancusi. The art he was producing focused on his experiences of being a black American, and many in Europe and America saw him as an important Modernist painter. In 1954, he married a dancer, Nanette Rohan.

When he first began painting, Bearden's style was influenced by the Mexican muralists who in the 1920s produced brilliantly colored wall paintings depicting their heritage, especially Diego Rivera and José Clemente Orozco. Then just after World War II, his religious-style paintings were more abstract. His art changed again during the 1960s, as he began making collages by cutting and tearing up magazine photographs, posters, and painted papers and using them to create art that expressed his vision of African American life in America. These colorful images include places in Harlem, trains, jazz and blues musicians, the rural American South, and African American religion and spirituality. They were described by a writer as "Patchwork Cubism." At that time, he helped to start another art group in Harlem called the Spiral, where he and others discussed the responsibility of African American artists in the struggle for civil rights.

Bearden had many pet cats. A heavily built man and almost six feet tall, he was incredibly gentle.

His cats included a tabby named Gypo that he found in the forest, Tuttle (short for Tutankhamen, the Egyptian pharaoh), Rusty (named after legendary Persian hero Rustam), and Mikie (short for Michelangelo, the Renaissance artist).

An avid reader, Bearden loved learning and his studio was crammed with books on poetry, philosophy, politics, mythology, religion, art, and ancient literature. He also wrote his own books and articles, especially about African American art and life.

Jazz and blues music was always important to Bearden. Many well-known jazz performers, such as Duke Ellington and Fats Waller, visited his home when he was a child. For 16 years, he worked in a studio above the Apollo Theatre in Harlem, famed for its lively African American acts.

Throughout his career, Bearden created lively works of art, inspired by a range of artists, including Duccio, Giotto, Pablo Picasso, and Henri Matisse, as well as African art, Chinese landscapes, and American life. Increasingly, his collages had musical themes, and he also designed costumes and stage sets for his wife Nanette's dance troupe and other troupes. In 1973, he and Nanette built a holiday home on the Caribbean island of Saint Martin, where Nanette's ancestors had lived.

Bearden spent his life making art and also helping African Americans become more equal in society. He received several awards, including the National Medal of Arts. In 1980, President Jimmy Carter held a White House reception for him. Bearden died in 1988 at the age of 76. Two years after his death, the Romare Bearden Foundation was established to help those who could not afford to study art.

FRANZ MARC

SEEING the WORLD THROUGH ANIMALS' EYES

F ranz Marc was born in 1880, in Munich,
Germany. He always loved animals, and he showed
promise as an artist. He joined the Munich
Academy of Art when he was 20. After completing
his training, he painted horses, dogs, cats,
monkeys, cows, and other animals in bright
colors and distorted shapes.

He believed that animals were the only innocent creatures in a damaged world, and his paintings of them expressed his feelings about the world leading up to World War I.

In 1903, he spent six months in Paris studying Impressionist and Post-Impressionist paintings, and after returning to Germany, he studied animal anatomy so he could draw them accurately, before distorting them in his paintings. He spent hours at the Berlin Zoo, studying and sketching the animals from all angles. His animals were recognizable, but they also symbolized his view of life through angled shapes and vivid colors.

Marc used colors symbolically. For him, blue was spiritual, yellow was happy and gentle, and red was angry and heavy. He and his friend Wassily Kandinsky started an artists' group called Der Blaue Reiter (The Blue Rider). Everyone in the group was invited to be expressive.

In about 1911, Marc
painted his pet dog
Ruthie. He also painted
several cats, sleeping

or grooming themselves. Their poses seem so
natural that it is likely he had pet cats, too. In
1914, he bought a house in Austria, where he lived
with his wife, his dog Ruthie, possibly cats, and
a tame deer.

Ruthie

He expressed the world as seen through animals'
eyes, and in 1915, he wrote an essay, *How Does a
Horse See the World?* He wrote, "Is there a more
mysterious idea for an artist than to imagine how
nature is reflected in the eyes of an animal?"

GEORGIA O'KEEFFE

AMERICAN MODERNIST

Georgia O'Keeffe preferred not to have people around as she created her huge paintings of natural forms, but she loved the company of her Siamese cats and her teddy bear–like chow dogs.

Georgia O'Keeffe is known internationally for her bold art, especially her large flower paintings. She is often called the Mother of American Modernism.

Born in 1887, the second of seven children, Georgia grew up on a dairy farm in Wisconsin, where there were cows, horses, dogs, and cats.

When she grew up, O'Keeffe had a Siamese cat, but she loved dogs too, and in the 1950s, she had a poodle named **Pancho**.

From early on, her mother encouraged her to study art, and she took watercolor lessons from a local artist, Sara Mann. At the time, it was unusual for families to encourage higher education for their daughters, but O'Keeffe's family was different, and in 1905, Georgia went to the Art Institute of Chicago, and from 1907, to the Art Students League in New York. There, through the influential artist-teacher William Merritt Chase, she learned the techniques of traditional painting. While at the Art Students League, she won the William Merritt Chase still life prize in 1908.

O'Keeffe's prize was a scholarship for the league's summer school in Lake George, New York, and while she was there, she visited an exhibition of watercolors by the French sculptor Auguste Rodin at Gallery 291, owned by the famous photographer Alfred Stieglitz.

Once O'Keeffe had finished studying, however, she decided she was not good enough to be able to earn a living as a painter. She took a job as a commercial artist in Chicago, drawing lace and embroidery for advertisements. She then contracted measles, which affected her eyesight. O'Keeffe moved back in with her mother and siblings in Virginia. She enrolled in the University of Virginia's summer school art classes, where she learned about the artistic theories of the artist Arthur Wesley Dow and particularly how to use line, color, and shading harmoniously.

O'Keeffe was attracted to the wild and open landscape around Amarillo in Texas, so she went there and taught art. As the surroundings were quite harsh, she taught her students to see  beauty in everything, saying they should draw what they loved. One day, one of her students brought his pony to class. O'Keeffe did not flinch, but encouraged everyone to draw it. It was unconventional actions like this that inspired her students and other teachers but angered the authorities that wanted her to follow strict lesson plans and art books. O'Keeffe believed that art students should express themselves individually rather than simply copy the work of the Old Masters, which was the traditional way of teaching art. She thought that students who could not relate to the times and places of past art would not learn from it.

In 1914, O'Keeffe attended Columbia Teachers College in New York City and once again took classes from Arthur Wesley Dow. His ideas had a powerful effect on her art. She did extremely well in the creative courses, but she struggled at academic subjects.

During the summer of 1915, O'Keeffe needed to earn money and she accepted another teaching position. In her spare time, she drew natural forms in charcoal, making them look different and unique. The following year, a friend sent some of these to Alfred Stieglitz. He immediately showed ten of them in his Gallery 291, although O'Keeffe did not know about this. Stieglitz was a central figure in making modern artists known in New York, and he loved O'Keeffe's drawings. He asked to see more of her work.

O'Keeffe was teaching in Canyon in Texas. It was a town smaller than Amarillo. She loved the colors of the skies and the nearby Palo Duro Canyon, and she spent time painting vibrant watercolors there. By then, she and Stieglitz were writing to each other regularly, and in the spring of 1917, he held her first solo exhibition. When she became ill with the flu, he suggested she move back to New York. As soon as she arrived, Stieglitz helped her find a place to stay, took many photographs of her, and helped to make her famous.

In January 1923, an exhibition of O'Keeffe's work at Gallery 291 attracted 500 people on the first day. She showed 100 watercolors, oil paintings, and charcoal drawings. As a woman in the modern art world, she attracted much attention.

After Stieglitz's first wife divorced him in 1924, he and O'Keeffe were married. Although Stieglitz was 23 years older than O'Keeffe, and he loved the city while she preferred the country, they both shared a love of art.

Soon after their marriage, O'Keeffe began to paint large canvases of brightly colored flowers. No one had ever painted huge flowers like these; they were clear and precise, and they made her famous.

O'Keeffe's flower paintings sold for high prices, and in 1925 she began to paint New York skyscrapers from her apartment on the 30th floor in the newly built Shelton Hotel in Manhattan, at the time, the tallest hotel in the world. She also spent time at the Stieglitz family house at Lake George, where she painted abstractions of the natural world. She became recognized as one of America's most important artists.

Because the landscape and architecture appealed to her, from 1929, O'Keeffe began spending summers alone in New Mexico. For the next 20 years, she spent a lot of time living and working there, away from New York and her husband. She loved exploring and painting the landscape, and just as she had challenged her students in Texas to see the beauty around them, she saw beauty everywhere, too.

Her fame continued to grow around the world. In 1940, she bought a house in New Mexico, where she was happy, even though it was isolated and had no running water, electricity, or phone. Later, she bought an abandoned house in the village of Abiquiu that had a large garden. In 1946, she flew back to New York to be with Stieglitz, who had suffered a stroke. He died that summer.

Among many awards, O'Keeffe was elected to the National Institute of Arts and Letters, a great honor for a female artist. She traveled abroad a bit, and her paintings became more abstract.

After O'Keeffe's poodle Pancho was tragically killed by a car, a neighbor gave her two chow puppies, which she named Bo  and Chia. From then on she always had pet chows, six in total during her life, including Bobo, Jingo, and Inca. When she was 85, she reported, "Jingo's a year and five months old now. It seems to be my mission in life to wait on a dog."

Sadly, O'Keeffe began losing her eyesight, and in 1972, she stopped painting, taking up pottery instead. She died in 1986, aged 98.

ANDY WARHOL

KING of POP ART

Eccentric, outgoing, and the most famous Pop artist of all time, Andy Warhol (and his mom) adored cats and lived with 25 of them. He also had dogs and was inseparable from Archie and Amos, his dachshunds.

One of the most famous Pop artists, Andy Warhol was born in Pittsburgh, Pennsylvania, in 1928. His real surname was Warhola, and his parents came from a village in Czechoslovakia (present-day Slovakia). Andy's mother, Julia, loved cats, and Andy grew up surrounded by feline friends in his early years. When Andy was six, his father bought a yellow brick house close to the Catholic church where they worshipped twice a week. One entire wall of the church glittered with golden icons—brightly colored, flat-looking pictures of holy figures. Later, Andy remembered how powerful these flat-looking, colorful pictures had been and made many of his own.

The youngest of three boys, Andy was often ill. When he was eight years old, Andy contracted Saint Vitus' Dance, or Sydenham's chorea, a disorder that meant he had to stay in bed for 10 weeks and left him with nervous tremors, a red mark across his cheek, and scarring. He grew up terribly embarrassed about himself. Over the following two summers, he fell ill again and could not go out to play with other children, instead staying at home, reading comics, and drawing with his mother and brothers. Julia was always drawing and making things, and she encouraged her children to draw and make things, too.

In 1942 when he was 14, Andy's father died unexpectedly after drinking poisoned water. Andy was overwhelmed, and his mother said he should not attend the funeral or it would make him ill again. For the rest of his life, Warhol had an obsessive fear of illness and death.

When he did go to school, Andy struggled with the work until at high school he became friends with a girl named Eleanor Simon who was like an older sister and helped him with his schoolwork. By the time he left school, he had excelled and had won a scholarship to receive drawing classes for gifted children at the Carnegie Institute at the Carnegie

Museum in Pittsburgh. One of his teachers later recalled, "From the very start, he was original." At the museum, Andy marveled at the ancient sculpture and architecture, and he met rich children at the classes.

In 1945, Warhol enrolled at Carnegie Institute of Technology to study for a degree in pictorial design. He made friends and took dancing classes, remembering later that he wanted to be a tap dancer. He graduated in 1949.

After graduating, Warhol moved to New York and worked as an illustrator for *Glamour*, *Vogue*, and *Harper's Bazaar* magazines. He became the most successful and highly paid commercial illustrator in New York. Because he dressed scruffily and carried his work in a paper bag rather than a briefcase, he was nicknamed "Raggedy Andy" and "Andy Paperbag."

To make his illustrations, Warhol drew simplified drawings then traced over them in ink. While the ink was still wet, he pressed more sheets of paper on top, making several copies. His pictures were fresh and a bit messy, contrasting with more common, neat advertising pictures.

In 1952, Warhol's mom moved to New York to look after her son. She dressed like a Czechoslovakian peasant, so Warhol took her shopping at Macy's department store, but she preferred her old clothes.

Warhol had a cat named Hester. He was concerned that she was lonely, so he brought home another cat to keep her company, and then he kept bringing more cats home—and he named them all Sam. Having a house full of cats inspired Warhol and his mother to work together on a book of hand-colored prints in 1954 called *25 Cats Name Sam and One Blue Pussy*. Julia had written the title, and she accidentally left off the "d" at the end of the word "Named," but Andy liked the mistake,

so he left it in the book's title. In 1957
they collaborated on a second book
called *Holy Cats*, which was full of
Julia's illustrations of cats and angels.

In the late 1950s, Warhol began making fine art
rather than commercial art. He and several other
artists of the time felt that art had become too
distanced from ordinary people and appealed to
only a small part of society. In London, a movement
called Pop Art had started; Pop artists made art
that everyone could understand and enjoy because
it was brightly colored and about subjects most
people saw every day, including advertising,
packaging, and pop stars. In 1960, Warhol began
using advertisements and comic strips in his
paintings—things that most people discarded.
There was a bit of a race among other artists to
produce a memorable Pop Art style. One day,
Warhol was chatting to the art dealer Muriel
Latow, who suggested that he paint things like
soup cans and dollar bills.

In 1960, Warhol bought a large townhouse on Lexington Avenue in Manhattan. Rather than "normal" furniture, he kept his collections there, including gumball machines, magazines, and art materials. He lived in the house with his mother and their many Siamese cats. Every morning at 5 am, his mother swept the street outside the house.

Warhol began producing images of everyday things, including Campbell's soup cans and Coca-Cola bottles. He also made images of movie stars. In 1962, he began making pictures with silkscreen printing methods, using stencils to transfer images. Until then, silkscreen had only been used in advertising. Warhol liked it because it removed the expressiveness of an artist's brushstrokes and could be reproduced hundreds of times, but his pictures never looked exactly the same. He used bright colors and made each one look a little bit messy.

In 1962, Warhol exhibited 32 of his Campbell's soup can images together. From 1964, he rented a studio that he painted silver and called the Factory. The name came from the idea that the studio worked like an actual factory where Warhol employed assistants to produce his silkscreen pictures, like an assembly line in a factory. He expanded into performance art, filmmaking, sculpture, and books. He also produced images of Hollywood celebrities, such as Marilyn Monroe and Elizabeth Taylor. From 1963 to 1976, he created approximately 600 films, lasting from a few minutes to 24 hours. A black and a white cat lived in the Factory.

After surviving a 1968 assassination attempt, Warhol distanced himself from the unconventional people who came to his studio. Instead, he mixed with wealthy people, and throughout most of the 1970s he produced portraits for them from Polaroid photographs.

In 1976, Warhol made a portrait of his friend's dachshund, **Maurice**.

Archie the dachshund joined Warhol's collection of pets in 1973. A few years later, Amos, another dachshund, joined Archie, and both dogs went everywhere with Warhol and appeared in his art.

Still fearful of illness and death, in 1987 Warhol went into the hospital for a routine operation. While there, he had a massive heart attack and died. He was 58.

Archie

Amos

SALVADOR DALÍ

SPANISH SURREALIST

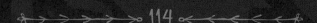

Salvador Dalí loved to shock
people. His painting style was smooth,
elegant, and surreal—and so were his
pet ocelots, who accompanied him
everywhere he went.

From an early age, the Spanish artist Salvador Dalí showed outstanding artistic skills. Born in Figueres, a small town outside Barcelona, in 1904 to a wealthy family, he had his first drawing lessons at age 10. As a teenager, he was inspired by Futurist paintings that showed things from several angles to capture a sense of movement. At 17, he was heartbroken when his mother died. He moved away, to Madrid to attend the Madrid School of Fine Arts, where he experimented with Impressionist and Pointillist styles. Three years later, he was expelled for insulting his teachers.

Meanwhile, he was already exhibiting his work locally and had discovered the work of artist Giorgio de Chirico, who painted nightmarish, odd scenes. Dalí also began studying the work of Sigmund Freud, the "Father of Psychoanalysis."

Freud explored the human mind. He wrote about our inner thoughts, which he said contain hidden truths and desires, and he described the mind as

being like an iceberg:
the tip of an iceberg, seen
above the surface of the
water, is a small fraction
of the whole thing. This is
like the conscious mind—
our awareness. Just below the
water is a larger part of the
iceberg, like our subconscious

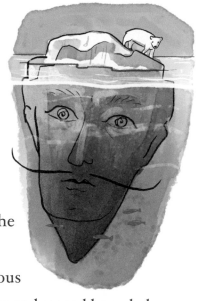

mind that contain memories and stored knowledge.
Finally, the largest part of the iceberg is deep under
the water, like the unconscious mind that we are
rarely aware of but that influences our judgments,
feelings, and behavior.

In 1926, Dalí (even he called himself Dalí and not
Salvador) moved to Paris, where he met Pablo
Picasso and became fascinated by Cubism.

Inspired by the 17th-century
painter Diego Velázquez, he
grew a long, curly moustache
that became his trademark.

In 1929 Dalí worked with the Spanish director Luis Buñuel to make a short, disturbing film about obsession called *Un Chien Andalou* (*An Andalusian Dog*), which made the Surrealists notice Dalí. Inspired by Freud's theories, Surrealism was an art movement that started in Paris in 1924. "Surreal" means "above real," and Surrealists expressed their inner thoughts and dreams through their art.

Dalí began making more films and extremely detailed and realistic paintings with bizarre and unexpected things happening in them, like dreams or nightmares. He described his paintings as "hand-painted dream photographs."

Dalí met Elena Ivanovna Diakonova, known as Gala, in August 1929. She was Russian, ten years older than Dalí, and at that time, married to the Surrealist poet Paul Éluard. She became Dalí's muse—he painted her often.

Dalí had some important exhibitions and was invited to join the Surrealist group that met in the Montparnasse quarter of Paris. They admired Dalí's way of expressing the subconscious in his paintings. His painting style was smooth and life-like, showing uncomfortable situations. He also put on art performances wearing strange costumes, and he made odd objects, such as a telephone with a lobster for its receiver.

After they met, Dalí and Gala became romantically linked, and Dalí's father was furious when he heard about it. He also saw his son's connection with the Surrealists as a bad influence on his Christian morals. They had a huge argument, and Dalí's father told him that he had to end his relationship with

Gala, but Dalí ignored him and the following summer, he and Gala rented a small fisherman's cabin together.

Over the years, Dalí bought the fisherman's cabin and other cabins around it, eventually turning them into one beautiful villa by the sea. He and Gala married in 1934, and his father reluctantly accepted her as his son's wife. In 1958, they remarried in a grand Catholic ceremony. Gala inspired many of Dalí's paintings. She also worked as his business manager, organizing their extravagant lifestyle—which eventually included using some rather exotic pets as accessories.

In Paris in 1969, Dalí was photographed walking an **anteater**.

In 1934, the art dealer Julien Levy introduced Dalí to the United States with an exhibition of his work in New York. It caused a sensation, and a special "Dalí Ball" was held in his honor. Later that year, he and Gala went to a masquerade party also in New York, but their costumes were extremely distasteful; they horrified his new admirers, and he had to apologize. He continued to shock people on purpose.

When he returned to Paris, Dalí began to have many arguments with the Surrealists, and in 1934, he was expelled from the Surrealist group, mainly because of differing views about art and politics.

Yet despite no longer being part of the group, Dalí continued painting in his Surrealist style, and he became the most famous Surrealist of all time. Many of his paintings were inspired by artists such as Gustave Courbet and Jan Vermeer, but his emotional themes and subjects remained as weird as ever. When German troops entered France in

1939 at the outbreak of World War II, he and Gala went to live in the United States.

Dalí seemed to become even more eccentric as time passed. He once said, "The only difference between me and a madman is that I am not mad."

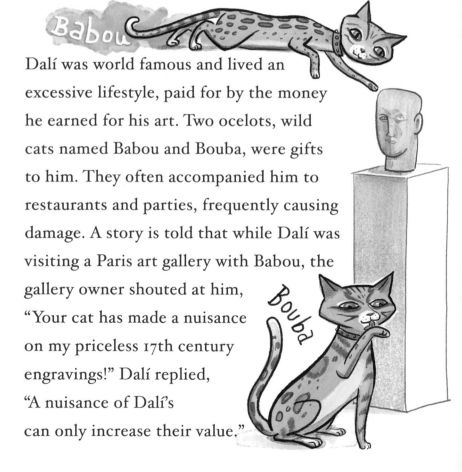

Dalí was world famous and lived an excessive lifestyle, paid for by the money he earned for his art. Two ocelots, wild cats named Babou and Bouba, were gifts to him. They often accompanied him to restaurants and parties, frequently causing damage. A story is told that while Dalí was visiting a Paris art gallery with Babou, the gallery owner shouted at him, "Your cat has made a nuisance on my priceless 17th century engravings!" Dalí replied, "A nuisance of Dalí's can only increase their value."

Dalí's early paintings were small,
but his art grew with his fame.
By the end of his career, he was
making paintings as tall as **giraffes**!

As well as painting, Dalí designed jewelry, advertising,
stage sets, furniture, and ballets; he made films and
sculptures, and he wrote and illustrated books.

In 1969, Dalí illustrated Lewis
Carroll's classic children's
story, *Alice in Wonderland*,
which gave him many
opportunities to draw
animals in a surreal way.

In 1945, Dalí worked with Alfred Hitchcock,
creating dreamlike sequences in the film
Spellbound. In 1971, the Dalí Museum opened in
Ohio, and in 1974, the Teatro-Museo Dalí opened
in Figueres. He died in Figueres in 1989, aged 85.

HENRI MATISSE

FRENCH WILD BEAST

Labeled a wild beast for his unnatural, vivid colors, Henri Matisse expressed himself with bold paintings and took his cats everywhere with him, from his studio to his expensive hotel rooms.

Along with Pablo Picasso and Marcel Duchamp, Henri Matisse was one of the most influential artists of the 20th century. Born in northern France in 1869, Henri's father, a wealthy grain merchant, encouraged him to become a lawyer. So when he was 20, he studied law in Paris and passed the exams with distinction. Then he had to spend months recovering at home from appendicitis. To cheer him up, his mother bought him a box of paints. Later, he said, "From the moment I held the box of colors in my hands, I knew this was my life." He decided to become an artist, and in 1891 he returned to Paris to study art but he failed the entrance exam to the prestigious École des Beaux-Arts.

Matisse loved animals all his life, especially **birds** and **cats**.

Matisse enrolled at the Académie Julian, where he was taught by the artist William-Adolphe Bouguereau, who was highly admired for his smooth, realistic painting style. However, Matisse found Bouguereau's teaching boring and tedious. He left after a year and joined the studio of Gustave Moreau instead. Moreau was an important Symbolist painter who encouraged his students to try new ideas. Both Bouguereau and Moreau taught students to draw models over and over again. Moreau said, "Colors must be thought, dreamed, imagined." Matisse took the entrance exam for the École des Beaux-Arts five times and eventually, he passed.

At first, Matisse painted traditional style still lifes and landscapes, influenced by artists such as Jean-Baptiste-Siméon Chardin and Édouard Manet, and by Japanese art.

In 1896, Matisse exhibited five paintings at the Société Nationale des Beaux-Arts. In 1896 and 1897, he visited the Australian painter John Peter

Russell on the island of Belle Île off the Brittany coast. Russell had studied with Vincent van Gogh and Henri de Toulouse-Lautrec and was also a friend of Claude Monet. He introduced Matisse to Impressionist ideas of painting with bright colors. After their meetings, Matisse's style changed completely.

While struggling to earn money, Matisse married his fiancée, Amélie Parayre, who worked as a hatmaker to support them both. She also often posed as his model. Amélie and Henri had two sons: Jean born in 1899 and Pierre in 1900. Matisse's daughter Marguerite, from a previous relationship, lived with them, too. Matisse painted Marguerite with a black cat. Through John Russell, Matisse met Camille Pissarro, the Impressionist, who advised him to go to London to study the paintings of J.M.W. Turner.

Marguerite

For their honeymoon, Henri and Amélie stayed
in London. Like Pissarro and Monet, Matisse was
inspired by Turner's atmospheric paintings and his
use of color. After London, Matisse visited sunny,
hot Corsica, and on his return to Paris
early in 1899, he discussed art ideas with
other artists, such as Albert Marquet,
whom he had met in Moreau's studio.

In May of 1905 Matisse went to Collioure in the
South of France and invited the artist André
Derain to join him. There, they created a new
style of painting using vivid colors and ignoring
shadows and perspective that made things look
3-D. At the end of the summer, Matisse took 15 oil
paintings, 40 watercolors, and over 100 drawings
back to Paris. He loved the light, colors, and
scenery in Collioure and returned to paint there
in the summers of 1906, 1907, 1911, and 1914.

Deciding that the official art exhibition held in
Paris was stuffy and old fashioned, Matisse and

his friends Georges Rouault, Derain, and Marquet organized the Salon d'Automne (Autumn Salon) in 1903, and in 1905, Matisse exhibited some of the work he had produced at Collioure at the Salon d'Automne, along with other artist friends, including Derain, Marquet, Maurice de Vlaminck, Rouault, and Georges Braque.

Most visitors were horrified by Matisse's new paintings. The colors were overly bright, and the pictures looked messy and unfinished. One critic wrote scornfully that the paintings looked like fauves, or wild beasts. The movement became called Fauvism, and Matisse was seen as the leader. Matisse also made sculptures of expressive figures.

Throughout his life, Matisse was intrigued by the power of color. Through paint, he explored ways that colors could inspire different feelings, and he wanted his art to inspire positive, happy feelings in viewers. Fauvism did not last long, and most Fauvists soon began painting in other ways, but Matisse continued painting with bold, bright, and unnatural colors using few lines and flat-looking shapes. He explained, "What I dream of is an art of balance, of purity and serenity...like a good armchair which provides relaxation."

Even though Pablo Picasso was 11 years younger than Matisse, they became good friends. Matisse was influenced by Picasso's art and by traveling. After he had visited Algeria and Morocco, Matisse painted more exotic subjects and colors. From 1911 to 1916, he painted several figures in rooms decorated with Eastern rugs and African ornaments, and later, he painted the dazzling light of southern France, where he lived.

Over his life, Matisse had many cats. Although he didn't paint them very often, he loved them very much. In 1917, he moved to Nice. His last home in Nice was the Hotel Regina, where royalty had stayed. Matisse took his cats to live with him even there.

During the 1940s, Matisse had two tabby cats, Minouche and Coussi, and a black cat named La Puce (the Flea). He often shared his morning brioche with La Puce.

Matisse also had a passion for birds (and especially doves), which began during the summer of 1936. Along the banks of the river Seine in Paris, he had seen songbirds and doves in cages for sale. He bought several and kept birds for the rest of his life.

After an illness in 1941, Matisse was confined to bed, so he began making paper collages. With assistants, he cut painted paper into shapes, then arranged them into lively compositions. His first cutouts were for stage sets and ballet costume designs in 1937–38.

His cats kept him company.

In 1948, Matisse designed stained-glass windows for the Rosary Chapel in Venice. In 1954, aged 84, he died of a heart attack. He had given Picasso the last of his fancy pigeons, which Picasso drew in a famous work, *The Dove of Peace*.

WASSILY KANDINSKY

FROM RUSSIA with COLOR

Lover of color, music, horses, and cats, Wassily Kandinsky painted one of the first abstract paintings. He painted with bold colors, played harmonious music...and kept pet cats.

A pioneer of abstract art, Wassily Kandinsky explored the effects of color through paint. He was a leader of new ideas, and his art changed from figurative paintings, of things that we all recognize from the real world, to abstract paintings that expressed his own symbolism and ideas with music. His art inspired many younger artists who came after him.

Kandinsky was born in 1866 in Moscow to well-educated, upper-class parents of mixed backgrounds, including Russian, Mongolian, and German. Most of his childhood was spent in the cosmopolitan city of Odessa. Noticing his son's gifts with music and art, his father enrolled him in private classes for drawing, piano, and cello. While in Italy with his family as a child, he was inspired by the architecture of Venice and Rome.

In 1889, while studying law and economics at the University of Moscow, Kandinsky was selected as part of a group to study the people in the Vologda district in northwestern Russia. He became fascinated by their folk art and the ways they decorated their houses. Those shapes and colors inspired him later. In 1893, he accepted a position on the university's law faculty to teach law.

Kandinsky had a condition called synesthesia. This meant that he saw colors in his mind when he heard music and other sounds. So despite being happy teaching law, he was always interested in color and art, and in 1896, he left his job and went to Germany to the art school of Anton Azbe in Munich for two years. He studied under Franz von Stuck at the Munich Academy of Fine Arts in 1900.

VASKE

Kandinsky loved cats, especially an orange tabby named **Vaske** (which means "wash" in Norwegian).

In 1901, with three other artists, Kandinsky started Phalanx, a modern artists' association that expanded to include an exhibitions group and art school. While teaching at the Phalanx School, he befriended a student, Gabriele Münter, who became his companion for the next 15 years. From 1903 to 1909, he and Gabriele traveled around Europe and to northern Africa. The colors and light inspired them both.

In Dresden, Germany, in 1905, artists including Emil Nolde, Ernst Ludwig Kirchner, Fritz Bleyl, and Karl Schmidt-Rottluff formed a group they called Die Brücke (The Bridge), suggesting a bridge between art of the past and of the future. They painted to express their negative feelings about the materialistic society they were living in. The art was direct and simplified, with distorted colors and jarring shapes, and it intrigued Kandinsky.

Kandinsky and his friend Franz Marc formed a group with seven other artists in 1911. They called

it Der Blaue Reiter (The Blue Rider), probably because Kandinsky and Marc loved horses and also considered the color blue to be spiritual. They all used bold, unexpected colors and shapes to express their emotions, and they held three exhibitions and published a manual called *The Blue Rider Almanac*. The *Almanac* included contemporary, primitive, and folk art, all things that were influencing Kandinsky's art at the time. Kandinsky also published an essay, "Concerning the Spiritual in Art," explaining his belief that art should project spiritual ideas through line, color, and composition.

Kandinsky was producing paintings that blended abstraction with the real world and were also spiritual. He gave many of them musical titles, such as *Composition*, *Harmony*, and *Improvisation*.

When Germany declared war on Russia in 1914, World War I broke out. It meant that all Russians in Germany had to leave, so Kandinsky returned to Russia. When Franz Marc was killed in combat, Der Blaue Reiter ended. Before returning to Moscow, Kandinsky and Gabriele Münter traveled to Switzerland and Sweden, but their relationship ended. He soon met and married Nina Andreevskaia, the daughter of a tsarist colonel. Back in Russia, he discovered the work of the Russian Constructivists and Suprematists.

In 1921, the architect Walter Gropius invited Kandinsky back to Germany to teach at the Bauhaus, which was an innovative art, architecture, and design school. He and Nina moved to Berlin, gaining German citizenship in 1928. Kandinsky taught his students his deep beliefs about art, including color theories and spiritualism in painting.

Reflecting the groundbreaking developments and designs being made in the Bauhaus, as well as Modernism that was developing across the world, while Kandinsky was teaching at the Bauhaus, his paintings became more geometric, featuring circles, semicircles, straight lines, squares, and triangles.

At the Bauhaus, the teachers all lived in specially built Modernist-style houses near the school. Kandinsky and Nina were neighbors with the Swiss painter Paul Klee and his wife Lily, and some years later, Nina wrote a book called *Kandinsky and I*. In it, she told how the Kandinskys and the Klees could see each other's cats in the windows of their Bauhaus houses.

Kandinsky was given his first solo exhibition in New York in 1923 by the Société Anonyme, an American art organization that sponsored lectures, concerts, publications, and exhibitions of modern art. Kandinsky was still teaching at the Bauhaus then, and in 1924, he, Klee, Alexei von Jawlensky, and Lyonel Feininger started a group to follow Der Blaue Reiter, which they called the Blaue Vier (Blue Four). Their painting styles were all different, but they set up the group in order to exhibit together, and they organized exhibitions of their work in Germany, America, and Mexico between 1925 and 1934.

Kandinsky's first one-man Parisian exhibition was held in 1929, and that year he also traveled to Belgium and the French Riviera. Another exhibition of his work was held in Paris in 1930.

In 1931, Kandinsky created wall decorations for an architectural exhibition in Berlin. The Bauhaus— and Kandinsky—had moved to Dessau. Meanwhile, the Nazis were rising in power, and in 1933, they closed the Bauhaus. So Kandinsky and Nina moved back to Berlin. His work at the time featured pictures, signs, symbols, and softer color, and it came to be called his romantic or concrete period, but 57 of his paintings were confiscated by the Nazis and labeled "degenerate art."

Eventually, the Kandinskys settled in Neuilly-sur-Seine, near Paris. He began blending ideas, creating curving, richly colored, slightly humorous paintings that contrast with his geometric Bauhaus period. In 1939, the year that World War II began, he became a French citizen. By then, his work was widely admired, particularly by Solomon R. Guggenheim, who planned to open a museum dedicated to avant-garde art. Kandinsky became known as "the patron saint of the Guggenheim."

DAVID HOCKNEY

BOLD BRIT

One of the leading artists of the 20th and 21st centuries, David Hockney constantly experiments with different subjects and materials. Among his most famous works is his book filled with paintings of his dogs.

The fourth of five children, David Hockney was born in 1937 and grew up in Bridlington, northern England, in a working-class family. At 11 he won a scholarship to Bradford Grammar School, but because he already wanted to be an artist, he deliberately failed his exams as only students with the lowest grades were allowed to study art. He left there at 16 and went to Bradford School of Art where, unlike his grammar school days, he worked extremely hard. He remembered, "I was there from nine in the morning till nine at night."

At 22, Hockney began studying at the Royal College of Art in London. There he met American artist R. B. Kitaj, who was studying art in England. Many of Kitaj's ideas influenced Hockney, and so did several important artists who visited the Royal College, including Francis Bacon and Peter Blake.

While still a student, along with Peter Blake (who became a good friend), Hockney showed his work in a London exhibition called Young Contemporaries.

It attracted a lot of positive attention, and when he left college, John Kasmin, a London art dealer, put on an exhibition of his work called David Hockney: Pictures with People In. It was a sellout, and Hockney became celebrated as a new and exciting young Pop artist, although he insisted that his art was not Pop Art.

From 1961 to 1963, Hockney created a series of images after some famous 18th-century pictures made by William Hogarth, called *A Rake's Progress*. Hogarth's pictures are amusing but underneath show how deceitful many wealthy people were at the time. Hockney produced 16 prints that tell a moral story about similar problems in the 20th century.

In 1969, Hockney made etchings to illustrate *Six Fairy Tales from the Brothers Grimm*.

After his first solo exhibition in London, Hockney went to Los Angeles, California, where he discovered the brilliant light and sunshine. He began using acrylics for the first time, using the bright colors to express what he saw. He also used vibrantly colored crayons. Over the next 40 years, he lived in California for most of the time, teaching at various universities, including Berkeley and UCLA.

In California, Hockney painted colorful images of swimming pools that give a great sense of peace, the shimmering heat, and sparkling light. Sometimes there's a hint of a person in the pictures, but nothing definite. He also painted many portraits of friends—bold pictures that in some ways are like traditional portraits, but in other ways are different and original. He also designed sets for the ballet, opera, and theater.

Before returning to Europe, Hockney went to New York and visited Andy Warhol's Factory. They became friends, and they both became famous.

From 1968, Hockney painted several double portraits, working from both photographs and direct observation. Usually one of the sitters looks at the other, who looks out of the painting. From 1970 to 1971, Hockney painted his friends, the fashion designer Ozzie Clark and his wife, textile designer Celia Birtwell. Sitting on Ozzie's lap is their white cat Blanche, but in the title, Hockney renamed Blanche "Percy," the name of one of Celia and Ozzie's other cats.

Blanche

From 1973 to 1975, Hockney lived in Paris, where he made a series of colorful artists' portraits in crayon. He drew each of them during one session of three or four hours. The artists included his friend Andy Warhol and the photographer Man Ray.

Hockney drove from New York to Los Angeles with a friend in 1976, and two years later he moved to Los Angeles, at first renting a house, and then buying it. By that time, he had tried out numerous art styles and techniques, including drawing, painting, and printing, and several successful exhibitions of his work had been held.

 In the 1980s, Hockney started making photo collages, taking quick photos with a Polaroid camera and then arranging them to create one layered image. In 1983, he began a series of self-portraits that show his outward appearance and his inner character.

Since the start of his career, Hockney has painted everything around him, including where he lives, still lifes of objects including packaging and tulips, and portraits of relatives and friends. From 1993, he also painted his two dachshunds, Stanley and Boodgie, in natural poses. Stanley was named after the 20th-century comic actor Stan Laurel. Boodgie was called Boodgie "because he looked like one." Hockney recalled, "When I got little Boodge he was very small. I put a bell round him so I knew where he was."

In 1998, Hockney published a book of paintings and drawings of Stanley and Boodgie called *Dog Days*. He said, "These two dear little creatures are my friends. They are intelligent, loving, comical, and often bored. They watch me work; I notice the warm shapes they make together, their sadness and their delights."

Later in the 1990s, Hockney produced several large-scale paintings of the landscapes near his house in America. At the beginning of the 21st century, he wrote a book about Old Master painters, following his research and belief that they used a form of camera to paint realistically. In 2002, he moved back to Bridlington in Yorkshire, England. That year, he painted a portrait of a friend, the artist Lucian Freud, and Freud painted a portrait of him.

In 2012, Hockney had a huge exhibition at London's Royal Academy. A Bigger Picture featured huge, brightly colored paintings inspired by the Yorkshire landscape where he had grown up and had moved back to after so many years in California. The exhibition also included some of

his recent iPad drawings and films he produced, using 18 cameras, that were displayed on several screens at once.

Hockney painted a **dog** on a **car** in 1995.

In 2013, Hockney had a slight stroke, and soon after, his studio assistant Dominic Elliott died suddenly. Sad and depressed, for several months Hockney did not paint at all. He returned to California for a show of his work in San Francisco.

One day, he took up his brushes again and painted his assistant Jean-Pierre Gonçalves de Lima (J-P), with his head in his hands, resembling an 1890 painting by Vincent van Gogh called *Sorrowing Old Man (At Eternity's Gate)*. After J-P's portrait, Hockney's energy returned. He painted a portrait of everyone who came into his studio, including friends, relatives, acquaintances, and assistants. Everyone sat on the same chair in the same lighting conditions, and each painting was completed in three days.

JACKSON POLLOCK

JACK the DRIPPER

American painter Jackson Pollock produced huge paintings on the floor...and tried not to splatter his beloved dogs with paint since they were always near him in the studio.

The leader of Abstract Expressionism, Jackson Pollock was nicknamed "Jack the Dripper" because of his original painting technique, which became known as Action Painting.

Born in 1912 in Wyoming, Jackson was the youngest of five brothers. When he was a baby, his father was a farmer, but he then became a land surveyor for the government. The family had to move often, and Jackson grew up mainly in Arizona and California. He later remembered going on surveying trips with his father and seeing Native American culture, especially sand paintings made on the ground with thin lines of colored sand.

As a boy, Jackson loved his dog, whose name was **Gyp**— short for "**Gypsy**."

As he grew up, Jackson had a terrible temper and other behavioral problems. He ended up being expelled from two high schools, but two of his brothers, Charles and Sanford, were studying to be artists, and they encouraged him to do the same.

In 1930, Jackson followed his brother Charles to New York City, where they both studied art with Thomas Hart Benton at the Art Students League. After meeting the Mexican muralist José Clemente Orozco, Pollock became inspired to paint large works, and then he watched Diego Rivera, another Mexican muralist, paint murals at New York's New Workers School. Three years later, he joined the experimental workshop of a third Mexican muralist, David Alfaro Siqueiros, where he tried pouring and flinging paint at a canvas.

From 1935 to 1945, the Federal Art Project was run by the US government to support the visual arts in America. Groups of artists created murals, sculptures, illustrations, posters, photography, theater sets, and paintings, all paid for by the government. Pollock was one of many artists employed by the Works Progress Administration (WPA) on this Federal Art Project.

Pollock worked on the WPA's Federal Art Project from 1938 to 1942. Meanwhile, he was suffering with depression and alcoholism, and that year, he began seeing a therapist who encouraged him to express himself through art.

Soon after his work with the Federal Art Project ended, Pollock met the wealthy art collector Peggy Guggenheim, who loved his painting style and exhibited several of his works in her gallery, called Art of This Century. She also put on Pollock's first solo exhibition there. In 1943, she commissioned him to create a mural for her home.

It so impressed the art critic Clement Greenberg that he became Pollock's strongest supporter.

Pollock had developed a dramatic, ambitious painting style that was abstract, expressive, colorful, and large. Greenberg frequently praised it in his writing, and it became know as Abstract Expressionism.

Soon Pollock was a successful artist, earning good money from his painting. He met another artist, Lenore (Lee) Krasner, in 1936. Like Guggenheim and Greenberg, she also loved his work. In 1945, they married. With Guggenheim's help, they bought a house and barn in a peaceful part of Long Island, New York, and they turned the barn into a studio. Krasner had a studio in the house, and Pollock worked in the barn.

In the barn, Pollock developed his unique painting method that gained him the nickname "Jack the Dripper." Using giant canvases laid on the floor, he dripped, threw, dribbled, and splattered paint on to the surface. The layers of paint resembled the trails of colored sand of the Native American art he saw as a boy, but his were more abstract and layered.

Gyp II

Ahab

Pollock always loved dogs, and in his studio, he was kept company by his two dogs, a border collie mix named Gyp and a standard poodle named Ahab. Gyp came to Pollock and Krasner in 1946, the year after they had moved into their house on Long Island, and he was named after Pollock's childhood pet. Ahab was given to them by their friend, fellow artist Alfonso Ossorio, in about 1952. Ossorio had Ahab's sister, Horla. The name Ahab came from Captain Ahab, a character in a 19th-century book by Herman Melville called *Moby Dick*. At the time, Pollock also had a black crow he called

Caw-Caw, who made everyone laugh by pecking holes in tubes of paint and stealing pegs from washing lines in nearby gardens.

The layered webs and veils of paint on Pollock's canvases were built up in energetic, rhythmic patterns. Using sticks, brushes, trowels, and even the paint tins themselves, he flung, flicked, and poured his paint intuitively, not thinking consciously about where he would place the marks, but letting his subconscious mind take over and not allowing anything but the paint to touch the canvas. The technique helped to lift his depression, and it created a completely new type of art that had never been made before. No one knows exactly why he created his drip technique, but it seems to have been a blend of many influences during his life, including Native American sand painting, Mexican muralism, Impressionism, and Surrealism as well as his therapy. The action and application was as important as the final painting.

At first, Pollock gave his huge paintings numbers, not titles, so that viewers would see them without associating them with other ideas. Photographs of them were published in fashion magazines like *Vogue*, so the public became aware of them. Later, Pollock gave some titles like *Autumn Rhythm* and *Lavender Mist*. He often used gloss enamel paints that he could buy in many places. They were more fluid than oil paints, but he also thinned them with turpentine. As they dried speedily, he could apply his layers quickly without the colors blurring into each other. In some paintings, he added broken glass, sand, and other odds and ends, and sometimes he applied the paint so thickly that it rippled as it dried. Although he painted intuitively—that is, without thinking consciously—mathematicians have analyzed his paintings and found similar proportions and ratios found in nature.

In 1949, *Life* magazine published an article titled, "Is Pollock the Greatest Living Painter in the United States?" Although the article did not answer the question, it made him one of the most famous artists in the world, and his paintings appeared in even more magazines.

He had a solo exhibition in 1950, and his work was also exhibited alongside the paintings of Arshile Gorky and Willem de Kooning in the prestigious Venice Biennale. By 1951, however, he was drinking alcohol again. He began producing less colorful paintings, often using black ink, sometimes suggesting figures in them, but they were disliked by critics and the public. He still continued making them until 1953, but he hardly painted in 1954. In the summer of 1956, he died after crashing his car while he was drunk. He was 44 years old.

RENÉ MAGRITTE

BELGIAN SURREALIST

Probably the most imitated artist of the 20th century, René Magritte painted odd things in strange places, but his dog Lou-Lou was always where you'd expect her to be— right next to him.

Although the Belgian artist René Magritte was an ordinary man and his paintings were of ordinary things, his art was quite extraordinary.

The eldest of three boys, René was born in Belgium in 1898. Not much is known about his childhood, but he began taking his first art lessons when he was 12 years old. In 1912, when he was 14, his mother drowned herself in a nearby river. Her body was discovered later, farther down the river. For years, René painted faces covered in cloth, which many believed was evidence that he had seen his mother's body, but he probably did not. He found the next few school years difficult, and when he was 18 in 1916, during World War I, he enrolled at the Académie des Beaux-Arts in Brussels, the Belgian capital.

Magritte did not enjoy the art lessons at the Académie des Beaux-Arts, but while there, he became interested in Futurism, Cubism, and Purism and particularly the art of the Cubists Jean Metzinger and Fernand Léger.

After military service, Magritte married his childhood sweetheart, Georgette Berger, in 1922. To earn money, he designed wallpaper and then posters. In 1925, he saw the work of Italian artist Giorgio de Chirico, who painted pictures of eerie streets and strange things in odd places. Inspired by the mysteriousness of the paintings, Magritte began painting his own pictures of unusual objects in unexpected places.

Magritte had an exhibition at the Galerie Le Centaure in Brussels in 1927. The gallery was also paying him a small income to display his paintings regularly. But the exhibition received terrible reviews, and Magritte became depressed. He moved to Paris, where he met the artists and writers of the Surrealist group.

In the 1920s, the research of psychologist Sigmund Freud inspired the Surrealist movement in art and literature. Rather than painting what they could see, Surrealists explored the subconscious mind.

Believing that dreams could often seem more real than real life, some Surrealists painted nightmare-like or dreamlike pictures. In Paris, Magritte began painting his own dreamlike images, creating mystifying scenes that expressed the subconscious mind, and he sometimes used words and phrases as well as pictures.

In 1929, Magritte painted a picture that has come to be seen as one of his masterpieces. In his

Ceci n'est pas une pipe.

smooth, realistic style, he painted a huge pipe and beneath it painted the words (in French), "This is not a pipe." He meant it is not a pipe because it is a painting of a pipe. He was pointing out that art is not real, no matter how lifelike it might look.

The idea captured the Surrealists' imagination, and Magritte painted several more paintings along the same lines that he called *The Treachery of Images*, meaning that pictures are false because they often pretend to be something real.

Magritte's paintings were full of interesting ideas that were admired by the other Surrealists—including Salvador Dalí—but they were not selling, and in July 1930, he returned to Brussels.

Back in Brussels in 1930, Magritte and his brother Paul formed Studio Dongo, an advertising agency. Meanwhile, Magritte continued painting and hoped that his art would begin selling.

Many birds and animals are featured in Magritte's paintings, including rabbits, a rhinoceros, and **lions**.

Unlike many other Surrealists, Magritte was quiet and shy. He believed that secrecy and unexplained ideas were more important to paint than things that are obvious, and so his art is often quite baffling.

In the late 1930s, Dalí introduced Magritte to Edward James, a poet and art collector who was interested in the Surrealist movement and had purchased several of Dalí's paintings. James had invited Dalí to London to help him decorate his new house with surreal furnishings. After meeting Magritte, James invited him to decorate his house, too. Magritte stayed with James during the first Surrealist exhibition in London. After that, James bought many of Magritte's paintings. Within a short time, his work was attracting attention across Europe and America. Soon he could afford to give up his advertising work. But just as he became successful, World War II broke out.

During World War II, the Germans occupied Brussels and Paris, and so Magritte lost touch with the Surrealists in Paris. To contrast with the depressing times, he began painting in bright colors. Lasting for a little over a year from 1943, this became known as his Renoir Period.

Once World War II ended in 1945, Magritte returned to his original style, but from 1947 to 1948, he tried another style that was messy  and used quick brushstrokes that was called his Cow Period. Apart from that, his smoothly painted, realistic-looking painting style hardly changed throughout his life. As well as painting strange situations, he also sometimes copied famous paintings but changed parts, making them quite odd-looking. His idea was to make viewers want to look closer and question what is real and what is not.

Over his life, Magritte became recognized for his day-night paintings, pictures of men in bowler hats (he usually wore one, too), faces wrapped in cloth, blue skies, giant apples and combs, birds, trains, and views from windows. To viewers, they are just intriguing images, but to Magritte, every object had a significant meaning.

By 1960, Magritte was world famous. He acted like an eccentric artist and wore his bowler hat when out walking with Georgette and their dog, Lou-Lou.

Lou-Lou

During their marriage, he and Georgette possibly had more than one dog, but Lou-Lou became famous. First, because she went almost everywhere with Magritte. Second, for inspiring a song, written by the famous musician Paul Simon after he saw a photo of Magritte, Georgette, and Lou-Lou in 1983. Simon wrote and performed the song, called "René and Georgette Magritte with Their Dog After the War." It was a Surrealistic song, describing Magritte and Georgette as being fans of a music style called doo-wop.

In the last years of his life, Magritte continued working, painting canvases and murals, and making sculptures. He died in 1967, one of the most famous Surrealists in the world.

LEONARDO
da VINCi
the
GREATEST MAESTRO

Leonardo da Vinci is famous for his paintings, such as *The Last Supper* and *Mona Lisa*, as well as for his inventions. He was also an animal lover at a time when people were not like we are today and did not usually consider animal rights or feelings.

Born in Florence, Italy, in 1452, Leonardo became extremely successful as a painter, sculptor, architect, inventor, scientist, and military engineer. His ideas about art have influenced many artists ever since and made him one of the most famous people of all time.

He showed early talents in drawing and kindness toward animals from his youngest days. From the age of 14, he was apprenticed to well-known artist Andrea del Verrocchio and learned a wide variety of skills, including metalworking, leather arts, carpentry, drawing, painting, and sculpting.

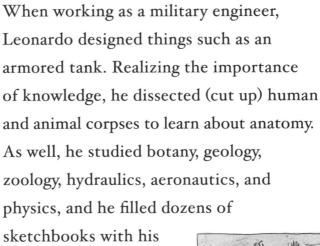

When working as a military engineer, Leonardo designed things such as an armored tank. Realizing the importance of knowledge, he dissected (cut up) human and animal corpses to learn about anatomy. As well, he studied botany, geology, zoology, hydraulics, aeronautics, and physics, and he filled dozens of sketchbooks with his drawings and notes under the themes of painting, architecture, mechanics, and anatomy.

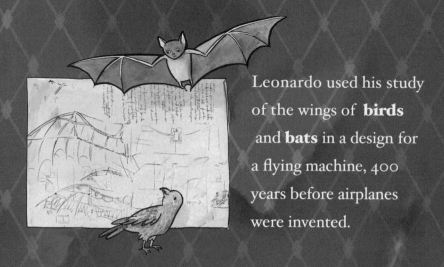

Leonardo used his study of the wings of **birds** and **bats** in a design for a flying machine, 400 years before airplanes were invented.

In the first life story written about him, the author Giorgio Vasari claimed that Leonardo loved animals so much that he bought several caged birds that were sold in Italy at the time mainly for food, sometimes as pets. But Leonardo opened the cages and let the birds fly away. Unusual for the time, he wrote that humans may be more powerful than other animals, but they are not better, and when most people ate meat, he was a vegetarian.

Sir

Edwin Landseer

Animal Lover

Sir Edwin Landseer

made the huge lion sculptures in London's Trafalgar Square. He also made paintings of animals, especially horses, dogs, and stags. He loved animals all his life and spent time with them, so he understood their moods and feelings. His paintings were commissioned by extremely rich people, and the less wealthy bought printed copies of them. Even Queen Victoria and Prince Albert asked him to paint their portraits with their pets.

One of Landseer's most recognized paintings is *Dignity and Impudence*, of his friend's dogs, Grafton the bloodhound and Scratch, a West Highland terrier. Landseer's paintings of dogs were so admired that the name "Landseer" has become the name for a type of black and white Newfoundland dog.

TSUGUHARU FOUJITA

CAT-OBSESSED ARTIST

Tsuguharu Foujita has been called "the most important Japanese artist working in the West during the 20th century," and he loved drawing and painting cats! In 1930, he published the *Book of Cats*, featuring 20 of his drawings of cats in all sorts of poses. It is often described as the most popular and desirable book on cats ever published.

Foujita studied art in Japan, then moved to Paris. He created Western-style paintings and prints using Japanese ink techniques and made many friends, including Henri Matisse and Pablo Picasso. Unusual for the time, Foujita had pierced ears, a wristwatch tattoo, and an ancient Egyptian hairstyle, and he often wore ancient Greek-style tunics and a lampshade on his head. He loved women, but he adored cats, and he became famous for painting them.

GLOSSARY

Abstract Expressionism
Expressive, usually abstract paintings, made during the 1940s through the 1960s.

Action Painting
A method of painting where artists throw, splatter, and drip paint onto canvases.

Art Nouveau
An international style of art, design, and architecture, created between 1890 and 1905, using curving lines and focusing on natural forms.

Cubism
A way of painting that aimed to show three dimensions on two-dimensional surfaces without using traditional methods of perspective.

Expressionism

Art that expressed strong feelings, often anxiety or anger, using colors, shapes, and distortions.

Fauvism

From 1905 to 1910, art made with vibrant colors and distorted shapes, capturing the natural world and expressing happiness.

Harlem Renaissance

During the 1920s through 1930s, black writers, artists, musicians, photographers, and scholars who lived in Harlem, NY, and had been oppressed in the South began expressing their talents in new, fresh ways.

Impressionism

In the late 19th century, beginning in France, some artists painted with vivid colors, using hardly any black, and applied quick brushstrokes to capture passing moments.

Pop Art

An art movement of the 1950s and 1960s that used images, ideas, and methods from popular culture.

Post-Impressionism

Several art styles created by artists soon after Impressionism, using bright colors and often their own symbols to show deeper meanings.

Surrealism

Art that explores dreams and unconscious thoughts.

~⁓ MORE BOOKS ABOUT ARTiSTS ⁓~

Anholt, Laurence. *Frida Kahlo and the Bravest Girl in the World*. Hauppauge, NY: Barron's Educational Series: 2016.

Carroll, Colleen. *How Artists See Animals: Mammal, Fish, Bird, Reptile*. New York, NY: Abbeville Kids, 1999.

duopress labs. *100 Pablo Picassos*. Baltimore, MD: Duopress LLC, 2016.

Editors of Phaidon Press. *The Arts Book for Children*. London, UK: Phaidon Press, 2005.

Hodge, Susie. *The Children's Interactive Story of Art: The Essential Guide to the World's Most Famous Artists and Painting*s. London, UK: Carlton Kids: 2016.

Stabler, David. *Kid Artists: True Tales of Childhood from Creative Legends*. Philadelphia, PA: Quirk Books, 2016.

Wenzel, Angela. *13 Artists Children Should Know*. Munich, Germany: Prestel, 2009.

⌁ ART CiTATiONS ⌁

Illustrator Violet Lemay has respectfully interpreted the paintings and artwork of the great artist to whom this book pays tribute.

Pablo Picasso: front cover *Reclining Woman Reading*, 1960; p 11 *The Rooster*, pastel on paper, 1938; *Buffet Henry II and Armchair with Dog*, 1959; p 13 *Clipper, Picasso's Dog*, 1895; p 15 *Les Demoiselles d'Avignon*, 1907; p 16 Costumes for *Parade* (performed by the Ballets Russes), 1917; p 17 *Woman Sitting Near a Window*, 1932; p 18 *Guernica*, 1937.

Frida Kahlo: p 21 *Self-Portrait with Monkey*, oil on masonite, 1938; p 23 *Untitled* (painted corset), paint on plaster cast, 1925; p 25 *Me and My Parrots*, 1941; p 26 *Self-Portrait with Thorn Necklace and Hummingbird*, 1940; *The Wounded Deer*, 1945; p 27 *Itzcuintli Dog with Me*, 1938.

Norman Rockwell: p 31 *Breaking Home Ties*, 1954; p 32 *Arrowheads* on the cover of *Boys' Life*, February 1952; p 37 *Little Spooners* on the cover of the *Saturday Evening Post*, 1926; p 38 *Freedom of Speech*, 1943.

Gustav Klimt: p 47 *Portrait of Adele Boch-Bauer I*, 1903-1904; p 49 *The Kiss*, 1907-1908; both are oil and gold leaf on canvas.

Paul Klee: p 51 *Cat and Bird*, 1928; *Red Balloon*, 1922; p 55 *Senecio*, 1922; *With the Brown Camel*, 1920; p 59 various drawings and paintings reproduced on the cover of *Il gatto cosmico di Paul Klee* ("Paul Klee's Cosmic Cat") by Marina Alberghini, 1896; *Cat and Bird*, 1928.

Suzanne Valadon: p 61 *Study of a Cat*, 1918; p 67 *Jeune Fille au Chat*, 1919; *Raminou*, 1922.

Ai Weiwei: p 1 (title page) *Untitled* (vase) from *Colored Vases*, 2007-2010, Han Dynasty vase and industrial paint; p 71 cat and dragon kites from the exhibit Er Xi (Child's Play), paper over bamboo, 2016; *Dropping a Han Dynasty Urn*, gelatin silver print (photograph), 1995;

Coca-Cola Vase, Han dynasty vase with industrial paint, 2009; p 72 *Forge*, installation of twisted rebar from schools destroyed in Sichuan's 2008 earthquake, 2012; p 76 *One Man Shoe*, wood board and leather, 1987; p 78, still frame from *Ai Weiwei: Never Sorry*, a documentary by Alison Klayman, 2012; *Cao (Grass)*, part of an exhibit of interlocking marble sculptures, 2015; p 79 section of kite from the exhibit Er Xi (Child's Play), paper over bamboo, 2016.

Romare Bearden: p 81 *Jazz Village*, mixed media collage on board, 1967; p 82 *Untitled (Woman and Rooster)*, watercolor and pencil on wove paper, circa 1978-1983; p 86 *He Is Arisen*, ink on paper, 1945; p 89 *Patchwork Quilt* (sketch), felt tip pen and ink on paper, and *Patchwork Quilt*, cut and pasted cloth and paper with synthetic polymer paint on composition board, 1970.

Franz Marc: p 91 *The First Animals*, 1913; p 92 *Elephant*, chalk on paper, 1907; p 93 *Dog Lying in the Snow,* 1911; *Blue Horses*, 1911.

Georgia O'Keeffe: front cover *It Was Blue and Green* in progress, oil on linen, 1960; p 95 *Jimson Weed/White Flower No 1*, 1932; p 100 *Drawing XIII*, charcoal on paper, 1915; p 102 *Ram's Head White Hollyhock and Little Hills*, 1935.

Andy Warhol: p 105 *Soup Cans*, synthetic polymer paint on canvas, 1962; p 110 cover art for *Holy Cats* by Julia Warhola, ink on paper, 1957; p 111 *Banana* in progress, screenprint in colors with collage, on wove paper applied to drawing board, circa 1966; p 112 *Untitled* from *Marilyn Monroe*, screenprint, 1967; p 113 *Portrait of Maurice,* 1976; *Archie* and *Amos*, both synthetic polymer paint and silkscreen ink on canvas, 1976.

Salvador Dalí: p 115 *Tuna Fishing (Homage to Meisonier)* in progress, 1966-1967; *Sleep*, 1937; p 118 *The Persistence of Memory*, 1931; p 122 **Ossip Zadkine**: *Head of a Man*, alabaster sculpture, 1924; p 123 *The Hallucinogenic Toreodor*, 1968-1970; *The Persistence of Memory*, 1931; *The Mock Turtle's Story* (illustration for Lewis Carroll's *Alice in Wonderland*), watercolor and ink on paper, 1969.

Henri Matisse: p 125 *Large Recling Nude (The Pink Nude)*, 1935; *The Piano Lesson*, 1916; *Madeline 1*, bronze sculpture, 1901; paper scraps from *The Parakeet and the Mermaid* in progress, gouache on paper, cut and pasted, and charcoal on white paper, 1952; p 128 *Marguerite with a Black Cat*, 1910; p 130 *Cat with Red Fish*, 1914; p 131 paper scraps and wall drawing from *The Parakeet and the Mermaid*.in progress, gouache on paper, cut and pasted, and charcoal on white paper, 1952 p 133 **Pablo Picasso**: *The Dove*, lithograph, 1949.

Wassily Kandinsky: p 135 *Compostion 8,* 1923; music notes taken from *Wedding March* from *Lohengrin* by Wagner, 1848 (arranged by K. Krantz); p 139 cover of *Der Blaue Reiter Almanac*, color woodcut, c. 1912; *Improvisation 19*, 1910; p 143 *Blue Rider*, oil on cardboard, 1903.

David Hockney: p 145 *A Bigger Splash,* acrylic on canvas, 1967; *Dog Painting 22* (from *Dog Paintings 1 to 45*), acrylic on canvas, 1993; p 147 *A Black Cat Leaping* from illustrations for *Six Fairy Tales from the Brothers Grimm*, etching with aquatint, 1969; p 149 *Mr. and Mrs. Clarke, and Percy,* acrylic on canvas, 1970-1971; p 150 *Self Portrait*, photocopy collage, 1986; p 152 *Patrick Steen's Cat on a Radiator*, digital (created on iPad), date unknown; p 153 *BMW Art Car No. 14*, enamel on BMW 850CSi, 1995.

Jackson Pollock: p 155 *Eyes in the Heat*, enamel on canvas, 1946; *Autumn Rhythm (Number Thirty)* in progress, enamel on canvas, 1950; p 158 *Mural,* enamel on canvas, 1948; p 163 *Life* magazine, August 8, 1949, including photos of three Pollock paintings 1) *Summertime 9A*, enamel on canvas, 1948, 2) title/date unknown, and 3) *Number 17A*, enamel on canvas, 1948.

René Magritte: p 165 *Spring*, 1965; p 167 *Georgette*, 1937; p 168 *The Treachery of Images*, 1928-1929; p 169 *Homesickness*, 1940; p 171 *Pom'po pom'po pon po pon po*, 1948; p 173 *Man in a Bowler Hat,* 1964.

Leonardo da Vinci: p 175 *Mona Lisa* in progress, oil on wood panel, circa 1517; p 176 *Birds in Flight*, ink on paper, circa 1505; *A Bear Walking*, silverpoint on paper, c. 1482-1485; p 177 *Glider*, media unknown, 1488.

Sir Edwin Landseer: p 179 *Dignity and Impudence*, 1839.

Tsuguharu Foujita: p 181 *Untitled* (cat) from *Book of Cats,* etching, 1930.

iNDeX

This book is an original work of authorship that explores, interprets, and pays tribute to the artists included in these pages. Illustrator Violet Lemay is one of the thousands of artists who have been inspired by the work of the artists in this book, in which she presents her own new and original works of art, all of which are reminiscent of various aspects of the artists' works. These images are used to familiarize the reader with certain iconic works for purposes of comment, criticism, and teaching. To assist the reader in exploring the artists' bodies of work, citations of these works can be found on pages 186–188.